Bill Haltom and Amanda Swanson

Full

HOW PAT SUMMITT, A HIGH SCHOOL BASKETBALL PLAYER,

Court

AND A LEGAL TEAM CHANGED THE GAME

Press

With a Foreword by
JOAN CRONAN

The University of Tennessee Press
KNOXVILLE

Library of Congress Cataloging-in-Publication Data

Names: Haltom, Bill, author. | Swanson, Amanda, author.
Title: Full court press : how Pat Summitt, a high school basketball player, and
a legal team changed the game / Bill Haltom and Amanda Swanson ; with a
foreword by Joan Cronan.
Description: First edition. | Knoxville : University of Tennessee Press,
[2018] | Includes bibliographical references and index. |
Identifiers: LCCN 2018011932 (print) | LCCN 2018026642 (ebook)
| ISBN 9781621904373 (pdf) | ISBN 9781621904366 (kindle)
| ISBN 9781621904359 (pbk.)
Subjects: LCSH: Cape, Victoria Anne.—Trials, litigation, etc.
| Tennessee Secondary School Athletic Association—Trials, litigation, etc.
| Summitt, Pat Head, 1952-2016. | Sex discrimination in sports—
United States—History. | Actions and defenses—Tennessee. |
Trials—Tennessee.
| United States. Education Amendments of 1972. Title IX.
| Basketball—Tennessee—History.
Classification: LCC KF228.C27 (ebook) | LCC KF228.C27 H35 2018 (print)
| DDC 344.73/099—dc23
LC record available at https://lccn.loc.gov/2018011932

The authors would like to dedicate
this book to Pamela Reeves,
who played high school basketball
in Tennessee, because the half-court line
might be the only obstacle in her life
she didn't blow past;
and to Charles Swanson,
because he never made
a distinction between
"women's sports" and "sports."

CONTENTS

ILLUSTRATIONS

I am an avid sports fan. I love the competition, physical prowess, and gritty determination of female athletes today. No matter the sport, fans are filling arenas, stadiums, and other sports venues to cheer for women. It wasn't always this way. As Women's Athletics Director Emeritus at the University of Tennessee, I can appreciate the story that is told in this book. The outcome made a difference in my life and the lives of millions of young girls who wanted to follow their dream.

What a nice description of the progression of women's basketball in the 1970s! Bill Haltom and Amanda Swanson paint a very accurate picture of the environment in women's athletics at that time.

The impact of the so-called women's movement and Title IX of the Health, Education, and Welfare Act are put into perspective by the unfolding case of a fifteen-year-old tenth-grader who had the strength to take on a system that clearly discriminated against female athletes — and, in the end, she received pivotal help from an unexpected source:

Pat Head Summitt, who became the legendary coach of the University of Tennessee Lady Vols. I had the privilege of working with Coach Summitt for over thirty years, and this book proves that integrity was perhaps her key quality, even at the beginning of her career. Haltom and Swanson tell the story in a powerful and gripping way.

These two authors took me on a fast and emotional ride down Memory Lane with the detailed and far-reaching story of Victoria Cape in Oak Ridge, Tennessee, in the mid-1970s.

The politics, pace, and the progression underscore the early years for me as a coach and athletics director for the Lady Volunteers. This strong story shows the power of courts, laws, media, and school administration in driving the implementation of new policy and creating a new culture.

JOAN CRONAN
January 2018

ACKNOWLEDGMENTS

We would like to thank Victoria Cape Hermes for sharing her story and her home; Charles Huddleston and Julia Brundige for their recollections; Don Ferguson for invaluable assistance with research and with finding photographs; Joan Cronan for her enthusiasm and support for the project; and our editor and copyeditor, Scot Danforth and Kathryn Little, for their hard work and wisdom.

Bill would also like to thank his partners at the Lewis Thomason firm, his personal assistant Sandy White, and his daughter Margaret Grace for her brilliant suggestion that he ask Amanda Swanson to become his co-author. And as always, Bill owes everything to his favorite reader, the love of his life, Claudia Swafford Haltom.

Finally, Amanda would like to thank Reedy, Judy, and Anna for their infinite tolerance for playing basketball in the driveway, and for everything else, too.

WAITING FOR THE BALL

Trish Head stood just inches from the half-court line, her hands on her hips, waiting patiently for the ball.

Well, not exactly.

Trish never waited patiently for anything.

The one thing Trish could not do was stand still, waiting. She was a whirlwind of energy and action, whether she was doing chores on the family farm, running from class to class at Ashland City High School, or racing her GTO at night down a country road.

And the one place where Trish was the most impatient was on a basketball court.

Trish didn't want to *watch* basketball. She wanted to play it. But on this January night in 1970, Trish was doing what she had to spend almost half of every game doing — watching other girls play the game she loved.

Trish wasn't watching from the bench. Trish never sat on the bench. She was watching from the court, standing as close as she could to the half-court line without crossing it, while three of her teammates and three of her opponents were playing the game on the other side of that line.

Trish hated that half-court line. She wanted to race across it, steal the ball from an opposing player, and then turn around and run the floor, scoring a basket at the opposite end of the gym.

But Trish knew that if she did, she would be called for a foul, and perhaps even a technical foul that could mean getting thrown out of the game.

Trish had to play by the rules, and in this case, the rules for Tennessee girls' high school basketball were made by the TSSAA, the Tennessee Secondary School Athletic Association.

The men (and they were all men) who made the rules for the TSSAA dictated that female high school basketball players in Tennessee could not play a full-court game. They could only play six-player (three forwards and three guards), split-court basketball. A team's three forwards would stay on one side of the court and be allowed to pass, shoot, and rebound. Meanwhile, the team's three guards would stay on the other half of the court and play only defense. Guards were not allowed to score or even set up plays. If they stole the ball from an opponent or rebounded, their only option was to get it back across half court and watch as their teammates passed and shot the ball.

The men of the TSSAA supposedly imposed the split-court rules for the safety of girls playing high school basketball in Tennessee. They firmly believed that unlike boys, girls simply weren't capable of engaging in vigorous physical activity like running eighty-four feet up and down a basketball court—or if they did, it could actually be dangerous to them. "Physical education experts" at the time argued that such "aggressive activity" by a young girl might cause her uterus to fall out. This was an actual concern, even though in the entire history of girls' high school basketball in Tennessee, no one had ever seen a uterus lying on a basketball court.

Trish thought the split-court rules were ridiculous. She had grown up playing full-court basketball, or more accurately, full-barn basketball.

Trish's father loved basketball, and he built Trish and her brothers a court in the hayloft of the barn on the Head family farm. Every night after chores, family dinner, and homework were done, Trish and her brothers would play full-barn basketball, racing from one end of the loft to the other, passing, shooting, rebounding, checking, and dispensing uncalled fouls.

That was the game Trish loved. But now as a forward on the Ashland City High School girls' team, she had to spend much of her time standing, watching, and waiting.

Of course, Trish knew that she was lucky to be playing girls' high school basketball at all, even confined to half the court. Her father had moved the Head family from Clarksdale to Ashland City when Trish started high school because Clarksdale High didn't even have a girls' basketball team. Had Trish grown up in Memphis (then the state's largest city), she may never have played the game at all, as Memphis had no girls' high school sports whatsoever. Just too dangerous, concluded the physical education experts.

So Trish waited, stuck until one of the guards on her team stole the ball or rebounded a missed shot or until the forward on the opposing team made a basket.

But Trish Head wouldn't always wait for the ball. She wouldn't always stay confined to half the court. Soon—very soon—she was going to race to the other end of basketball courts across the state of Tennessee, across the nation, and even across the world.

Trish Head, later known as Coach Pat Summitt, was going to take the ball and help change the game: not just for herself, but for every young woman in America.

THE GAME

The game that Trish Head was playing at her Tennessee high school in the 60s and 70s bore at best a family resemblance to what we think of as basketball now. Each team played with six players on the court, three forwards and three guards. If the modern game is increasingly defined by positionless play and versatility, this version of basketball was about as un-modern as it gets. Not only were the roles of forwards and guards assigned ahead of time; they also literally dictated which activities a player could participate in on the court.

Forwards handled the ball and shot on the other team's basket on one half court, while guards played defense on the other half court. The closest thing to a fast break was a defender passing the ball across the center line—which no player could cross—to her teammate on the other side. As a result of this two-court style of play, a guard could go her entire career without ever once putting a ball through a basket during a basketball game.

Of course, while having twelve players on the court may seem excessive by contemporary standards, it's nothing compared to how the game was played when it was first invented. In fact, James Naismith's original thirteen rules of the sport were entirely silent on the subject of how many players there should be, leaving players and schools to figure it out for themselves. In those early days, games were played with anywhere from three to fifty players per team, with both men and women playing according to the same hazy sets of rules, trying to put a soccer ball into a peach basket nailed to the wall.

It wasn't until an 1899 conference of physical educators formed a National Rules Committee that the game was officially modified and (more or less) standardized for women. The committee—whose members were all women—determined that not just two divisions of the court, but *three*, were necessary to "lessen the tax on the individual players when on a large floor." This same committee sought to eliminate "star playing" and "undue physical exertion," fearful of the effects either could have on the feminine psyche or physique. When later rule revisions instituted the two-court game, it wasn't because of a growing understanding that women were capable of running; it was to increase team play by maximizing spacing on the floor.

In fact, pretty much none of the early rule changes to women's basketball were guided by the hope of achieving athletic excellence, or even providing the best possible exercise program. As resolved by the Second Annual Congress of the Playground Association of America in 1908, the point of women's basketball was and should be "fun and the joy of recreation." It was widely hoped that that spirit would "save . . . the girls' sport from the evils [of competition] that have befallen the men's sports."

In Tennessee, high school girls playing basketball—whether for joy or competition—goes back to the early 1920s. Starting in 1925, the sport in high schools fell under the administration of the Tennessee Secondary School Athletic Association (TSSAA), a non-profit organized by school officials to oversee sports and interscholastic competition in schools. As the TSSAA began administering girls' basketball tournaments in the state under the split-court rules, they were operating according to contemporary wisdom regarding female participation in athletics. And that contemporary wisdom was summed up by the National Amateur Athletic Federation's 1923 resolution that the goal of sports for girls should be to maximize participation, even to the detriment of more athletically gifted students. Officials insisted that girls were to play sports "for play's sake," and for play's sake alone.

It wasn't until decades later that the grip of that philosophy on sports for girls began to slip at all. At the 1969 annual meeting of the DGWS-AAU Basketball Rules Committee—the latest in a long line of organizations trying to make its mark on the rules of basketball—they took the radical step of suggesting that women's teams might be able to "experiment with" the single-court, five-player game that we know today.

Even as some parts of the basketball world were easing into the five-player game for girls in high school, Tennessee was still clinging to tradition. They had good reason: tradition had been kind to Tennessee. The Amateur Athletic Union had started holding women's basketball tournaments in the early 1920s, and the league thrived in rural areas like the Midwest, Texas, and Tennessee. The AAU didn't share early rule committees' disdain for competition—they encouraged it—but they still used the split-court, six-player game for official competition. (Unlike in high school ball, they did allow for a "rover" starting in the 1930s. The rover could cross the half-court line to allow for fast breaks, but other players remained marooned on their respective sides of the court.)

For much of the fifty-odd years that the AAU was holding national women's tournaments, Tennessee teams ran the table. The Vultee Bomberettes out of Nashville won the state's first national championship in 1944, repeated in 1945, and won three more times that decade under different sponsorship. In 1950, they passed the torch to arguably the greatest AAU team in the league's history: Nashville Business College. NBC, or "NaBuCo," as acolytes called it, won eleven national AAU women's championships in twenty years, bringing attention to women's basketball across the state and building a loyal and proud fan base for the six-player game as they went.

As chance would have it, the end of NBC's dominance coincided exactly with the AAU's transition to the (traditionally men's) five-player rules. NBC won their last national championship in 1969, the same year that the AAU experimentally adopted the full-court game. They would adopt the five-player game officially in 1971.

There's little reason in the historical record to think that this was anything more than a coincidence—that Nashville's dynasty began to crumble at the same moment that the AAU began its move into the modern era. But still: it would be easy to understand how the diehard supporters of women's basketball in Tennessee—supporters that years of AAU national dominance had cultivated—could feel that the two phenomena were somehow linked. And so it would be easy to understand how those same supporters—concentrated in middle Tennessee, around Nashville, where the TSSAA was headquartered—might start to fear that the changing tides in the game were coming to sweep away the legacy they had only just built.

2

THE LAW

As the 1970s dawned, those same tides of change that were sweeping through amateur women's basketball were crashing down in the nation's capital. That's because in 1972, Congress passed Title IX of the Education Amendments of 1972, introduced by Senator Birch Bayh of Indiana and Representative Edith Green of Oregon.

Today, "Title IX" has, so to speak, gone generic. It's used as a kind of catchall phrase to describe progress in women's athletics, or the controversy surrounding progress in women's athletics, or the frustrating lack of progress in women's athletics—which is why it might come as a surprise to many that Title IX doesn't specifically mention athletics at all. It simply says, "No person in the United States shall, on the basis of sex, be excluded from participation in, be denied the benefits of, or be subjected to discrimination under any education program or activity receiving Federal financial assistance."

If it seems less than immediately obvious that those words would transform the sports landscape for decades to come, that's exactly how Edith Green wanted it. Bernice Sandler, a women's rights activist who helped draft the language of the amendments, has said that Congresswoman Green instructed Title IX supporters *not* to lobby for it, because then it might occur to someone how impactful the language could really be.

Eventually, those capabilities would become clear: the law would be applied to require equity in facilities, coaching, and resources for men's and women's teams in any school receiving federal funds. And as the reach of the law became more apparent, the controversy would follow. A number of congressmen either condemned Title IX in its entirety, or merely as it pertained to sports, while others introduced measures to try and limit its application to athletics.

But any congressional opposition to Title IX paled in comparison to the resistance in the athletic world itself. The NCAA paid close attention as the Department of Health, Education, and Welfare (HEW) worked to create regulations that would determine how Title IX would ultimately be implemented. The chair of the NCAA Legislative Committee, Robert C. James, insisted that whatever regulations they issued were likely to be "frequently disruptive, often destructive and surely counter-productive to the very objectives which Title IX seeks to attain."

James's statements on behalf of the NCAA proved to be a kind of call to arms, leading school and athletic administrators to take up their pens and phones in opposition to the implementation of Title IX. And while the HEW itself was largely unresponsive to this flurry of activity, Congress was not.

In May 1974, Senator John G. Tower, a Republican from Texas, sponsored an amendment to the education legislation that would exclude revenue-producing sports from the government's equality requirements. The amendment quickly passed in the Senate, to the glee of the NCAA's executive director Walter Byers. Byers sent a grateful note to Senator Tower, writing, "We thank you for your leadership in protecting the intercollegiate athletic programs of the colleges of this nation."

Fortunately for Title IX's supporters, Senator Tower's amendment was removed from the legislation during a joint House-Senate conference session. The NCAA responded poorly to this setback, blaming lobbyists like the Women's Equity Action League for swaying congressional opinion.

And NCAA officials weren't the only ones who resented the feminist activism they perceived to be behind the act and its accompanying regulations; even some within the

HEW itself were trying to avoid controversy by pointing fingers at outside forces. An AP story from November 1974 quotes Lou Mathis, the director of public affairs for the HEW's civil rights division, as saying, "We didn't initiate this law. That was done by women's pressure groups to Congress. But now the NCAA and all the athletic directors are saying we're trying to destroy college athletics. Well, we're not. All we're doing is enforcing the law. Why don't they attack the constitution?"

While the attacks that Mathis complained about almost certainly had roots that grew at least partly in misogynistic soil, administrators were able to point to a much more palatable reason for their concerns: money. They painted Title IX as instituting a zero-sum regime of austerity that would cripple previously successful men's sports on campuses, all to give women the right to do something they had no business doing in the first place. As Brigham Young athletic director Stan Watts put it to the AP for that same November 1974 story, "It would really put us in a financial bind if we were required to give equal opportunities to women."

Gwen Gregory, a lawyer for the HEW who was primarily responsible for coming up with the Title IX regulations, was forced to defend against alarmist claims like these. "We are not trying to destroy athletics," she insisted. "We are just saying you can't discriminate. We are not requiring equal expenditures; we are requiring equal opportunities."

Nevertheless, legal and political clashes surrounding Title IX would continue to reverberate for decades to come.

But the truth is, those clashes wouldn't matter too much for young Victoria Cape, a junior on the girls' basketball team at Oak Ridge High School in Oak Ridge, Tennessee. When Tennessee was about to grapple with the past and present of women's basketball—the moment that Victoria was about to find herself thrown into—the legal implications of Title IX were still too new, too unsettled, to push history too far in one direction or the other.

But what would be important—to Victoria Cape and her teammates, to Trish Head and her young program at the University of Tennessee, and to countless others—would be the *cultural* implications of the amendments. Women playing basketball in the 1970s had come up through the tradition of "play for play's sake," of shielding young female flowers from the competitive demons that drove men's sports, of a split-court game that was designed to keep girls safe instead of making them strive.

Title IX—no matter how controversial it was—was an official rejection of all of that. It was the United States government blowing up the centuries-old understanding that not only *were* women's sports different from men's, but that they *should* be different. It wasn't equality—not by a long shot—but it was a legal framework for how equality could be painstakingly, procedurally pursued.

Simply put: it was a start.

3

THE NON-SHOOTING GUARD

In 1976, fifteen-year-old Victoria Cape was an unlikely revolutionary. The daughter of academics, Victoria was bright, rational, and non-confrontational. She naively thought that when presented with the facts, people would do the right thing, on or off a basketball court.

Her father, James Cape, was a scientist with the Atomic Energy Commission in Oak Ridge, Tennessee, serving as a manager of the Office of Scientific and Technical Information. He was active in the arts, politics, and community sports, and he rounded out his Renaissance-man skill set with an effective tennis serve and a formidable bridge game.

Victoria's mother, Nancy Carolyn Barker, was a community activist who loved being in the arena, whether it was the world of Republican politics or the stage of her local theater. She was outspoken, but she was also an effective listener who believed that when people come together to discuss issues, they will reach the right result.

Like many loving daughters, Victoria thought her parents were perfect. She concedes now that perhaps they were a little *too* perfect for each other; they divorced when Victoria was five years old. Following their divorce, Victoria spent her childhood with her mother, first in Maryland, then in Hixson, Tennessee. When Victoria was fourteen, her mother planned to move from Hixson to Florida, and Victoria asked instead to join her father in Oak Ridge.

When she first arrived in Hixson, Victoria's only basketball experience came from playing outside on dirt courts with her siblings and friends in Maryland. But she was tall, and that was enough for a middle school assistant principal in Hixson passing her in the hallway.

"Do you play basketball?" he asked her, an interrogation that rings familiar to tall students across the nation, regardless of their athletic prowess. When she told him she didn't, he figured he'd take care of that, responding, "I want to see you at tryouts." By Victoria's own account, she wasn't an exceptional player, but she made the team and continued to play in high school when she went to live with her father in Oak Ridge.

In Maryland, the half-court game was long gone. And so when she arrived at Hixson Middle School, Victoria was at a loss to understand the strange half-court rule. When she came to Oak Ridge, what had been a curiosity for Victoria was quickly deemed a nuisance by her father.

James Cape was no stranger to basketball. He'd played in high school in Milford, Michigan, and a post-high school growth spurt left him standing six feet, six inches tall. His newfound height helped him earn a walk-on spot at the University of Michigan (a spot he would eventually relinquish in favor of his studies). So when his daughter told him she would be following in his basketball footsteps, he expected she would be playing *basketball*: the full-court, five-player game he had played at Michigan and watched at the University of Tennessee.

He could not believe his daughter wouldn't be allowed to cross half court. He was even more chagrined when Victoria was assigned to be a guard, meaning she would only play defense and rebound, and never once be allowed to shoot the ball.

James Cape was determined to rectify the situation. Like his daughter, he wasn't any sort of firebrand on the warpath; instead, he sought to discuss and resolve situations rationally. Victoria later recalled him as "one of those people who wrote letters to the editor," which is exactly the approach he took when confronted with the bizarre game masquerading as basketball in his daughter's school.

James wrote a letter to the TSSAA in Nashville, explaining his position. According to Victoria's recollection, the letter expressed a polite interest in seeing the rules of the game played in Tennessee changed to match those followed by most of the rest of the country. He contended that the current rules kept Tennessee women from being marketable to colleges nationally for possible basketball scholarships, and he asked what the TSSAA planned on doing about this.

That was meant to be the end of it. James Cape was confident that the TSSAA would respond favorably as soon as the error of their ways was brought to their attention. And a few days after sending his letter, James Cape got a response from the TSSAA that initially confirmed his optimism: the TSSAA promised to vote on the issue at their upcoming meeting. The Capes, perhaps overestimating the speed at which progress marches when left to its own devices, believed that would be that.

Of course, progress being what it is, the TSSAA didn't vote to make the change; they were entirely unmoved by James Cape's argument about the marketability of the state's female student athletes. But still, James was determined to force the TSSAA to do the right thing by his daughter and by all of the young female athletes on the Oak Ridge High School basketball team and on other girls' teams across the state. He sat down with Victoria and suggested they consider doing something unprecedented for the Cape family: file a lawsuit.

James Cape explained to his daughter that he knew a local attorney he had met though his involvement with the

Oak Ridge League of Women Voters and that they should talk with her about bringing a lawsuit.

Victoria responded quickly: "Let's do it."

She was really telling her father what she thought he wanted to hear. The truth was that Victoria was scared of the whole thing: of rocking the boat, of the idea of a real lawsuit in a real court, and most of all of the resistance she intuitively knew it would create.

But even as a fifteen-year-old kid, Victoria understood there was something more at stake than her own fear of conflict. She knew she was never going to be a college basketball star, even if she did get the rules changed.

Instead, she was steadied by a conviction—nurtured and shared by her father—that changing the rules was simply the right thing to do. She may have been scared to start a fight, but she was able to see past her own fear to the bigger picture.

"The whole thing was driven by a principle," Victoria later recalled. "Women should be playing the full court like guys. We should play the sport and that's all it is. It was as simple as that."

4

THE COACH

On the surface, it appeared that a young woman named Patricia Head was everything Victoria Cape wasn't. Born in 1952, Trisha—as she was called back then—was a fighter from day one. Her life began in a log cabin in Oak Plains, Tennessee, where there was no running water. After that came a farm in Montgomery County, where her days revolved around a backbreaking schedule of work, the daily chores every kid growing up on a family farm has to learn to do, rain or shine, through blistering heat or freezing cold.

The younger sister of three boys, she was always pushing to meet—then exceed—the standards set for people older, taller, and stronger than she was.

Where Victoria's parents were academics, Pat Head's were the furthest thing from it. Her mother Hazel Albright left school in the ninth grade to work. Her father Richard Head had to sell a mule to get the money to marry Hazel.

But Trish and Victoria came to basketball in surprisingly similar ways, even if they approached it differently after they arrived. Like Victoria, whose earliest memories of the game revolve around playing on a dirt court with her siblings in Maryland, Pat's basketball experience started as a family affair outside their home. But instead of dirt, she was playing on a makeshift court in the barn's hayloft, challenging her older brothers, refusing to go back into the house at night until she was on the winning team.

It was Pat's father who had built that court in the hayloft, because like James Cape, he had his own history with the sport. But unlike James, Richard Head never played for an NCAA team like the University of Michigan. Instead, the local Methodist basketball league was one of the few indulgences he allowed himself outside of work, before the farm became too demanding to allow for it any longer. But even then, basketball remained one of the only diversions from the hard work of daily farm life that he sanctioned for his children, which led him to construct their hayloft gymnasium and overlook the roughhousing that went on there.

In that hayloft, Pat blossomed into a skilled player and a fierce competitor. No doubt that competitive fire would have set her apart from a young Victoria Cape: for Victoria, the game was an integral part of a balanced education; for

Pat, the game was a war against the outer limits of what was possible, and losing wasn't an option. But still, despite their divergent philosophies, they were brought to the door of organized basketball in the same fashion: through the urging of an observant school principal. Like the administrator who pushed lanky Victoria into tryouts, Pat's elementary school principal knew a good thing when he saw one. Though Pat was only in third grade at the time, the principal directed her to start practicing with the eighth grade team right away.

Of course, at that Tennessee elementary school, the game Pat was playing was half-court. Pat described that version of the sport as "a strange, inhibited half-court game." Even though she spent her days doing the work of grown men on the farm and her nights beating growing men at two-on-two, at school she was confined to forty-two paltry feet of court. It was like telling Beethoven he could only use the keys on the left side of a piano, or Aretha Franklin that she would have to make do with just two of her available four octaves.

Pat resented it tremendously. Looking back, she wrote in her autobiography *Sum It Up*, "Gym teachers in those days didn't believe girls were capable of running full court—we were capable of heavy farm work, and of absorbing whippings, but for some reason, they didn't think we could run eighty-four feet without getting the vapors and passing out, or damaging our ovaries."

Even so, Pat soon came to realize she was lucky to have even that "strange, inhibited" version of basketball so readily available to her. This truth was brought into stark relief as she prepared to transition into high school. The school she was zoned for in Montgomery County not only didn't trust girls to run the full court; they didn't have girls' basketball at all.

For most families, that probably would have been the end of the story. To change which high school Pat had to attend, the family would have to leave behind the comfortable farmhouse they had only just finished building, not to mention the farm itself. In a time when it was hardly the norm for family patriarchs to support women's academic or professional goals—much less their athletic ones—no one would have blamed Richard Head if he had told his daughter that she would simply have to make do with the hoop in the hayloft for the foreseeable future.

Fortunately, Richard Head was not someone who was terribly concerned with the norms of the time. Faced with sending his basketball prodigy to a school with no basketball, his response, as Pat remembers, was simple and direct: "Well. We'll just move."

And move they did. The entire family picked up and relocated from their sturdy brick home to a rundown fixer-upper across the county line into Henrietta, clearing the way for Pat to attend Ashland City High School, which had a girls' varsity basketball team. In many ways, this would prove to be maybe the most important thing Pat and Victoria had in common, including basketball: the support of their fathers. James Cape was the thinking man who set pen to paper to open doors for his daughter; Richard Head was a laboring man who didn't always have a way with words but could say plenty with the force of his actions. ("He never told my brothers and me that he loved us," Pat would recall, "but every night, he put it on the table.") They were very different men, but they both found ways to be forces propelling their daughters instead of anchors holding them down.

Moving wasn't the last sacrifice the Head family would make for Pat's career. When it came time for her to go to college, there were no athletic scholarships to be had for women. That meant that the Heads would pay Pat's tuition at the University of Tennessee at Martin in full so she could get her education and follow the game that she loved.

And just as college brought more sacrifices, it also brought more reminders that the world saw women's athletics as different — as *less* — than men's. The women's athletic director at UT Martin, Bettye Giles, had a total budget of $500 for three sports. The basketball program, which of course was still firmly set in Tennessee's half-court ways, was in its infancy when Pat arrived. In fact, it was still considered intramural until just a year before. In Pat's first year, they went 16–3; their reward was to be invited *as guests* to the men's awards banquet, where the men celebrated a 3–20 season.

Like Pat and Victoria themselves, these fledgling programs often garnered more support from team fathers than they did from school administrators. Pat wrote, "At Martin's games, you'd see our dads sidle up to Bettye Giles and press bills in her hand, to help feed us or pay for our gas. My father was one of them. On more than one occasion, Richard slipped a hundred-dollar bill into the purse of Miss Giles." These paternal donations were supplemented by all manner of industrious efforts on the part of the players themselves: bake sales, car washes, raffles.

Even in this constraining environment, Pat set herself apart. According to her teammate Julia Brundige, Pat was less player than coach from the get-go.

"From the day she first walked into the UT Martin gym as a freshman, she was our leader both on and off the court," Julia recalled. "She even got us uniforms. Prior to Pat's arrival, we wore 'UT Physical Education Department' t-shirts with numbers taped on the back. Pat wouldn't stand for that, and so we got real basketball jerseys and shorts."

Julia remembers a time when she was being manhandled by an opposing player. Pat told her she had better either get back on the court and deal the offender a bloody nose, or she had better turn around and head for the bench. Julia committed the hard foul, and she was running so hot from the fire Pat lit under her that when the referee tried to reclaim the ball, she trembled, clenched her fists, and then unceremoniously threw the ball halfway into the stands.

Luckily for Pat, she didn't have to limit that fire to a contained version of the game for very long. Change came more quickly at the collegiate level than it did in Tennessee's high schools; it turns out a little incentive went a long way with universities' male administrators.

In 1972, female administrators formed the Association of Intercollegiate Athletics for Women, which established a basketball tournament that was the precursor to the NCAA women's tournament. That same year, it was announced that women's basketball would be an Olympic sport at the 1976 Summer Games. According to Pat, these new opportunities for meaningful victories helped push colleges to value women's athletics. That meant universities still clinging to the split-court past—like UT Martin had been—fell over themselves to start playing the prestigious five-player game.

Pat was determined to experience the full benefit of the change. She set her sights on the Olympic Games and began teaching herself the full-court game, starting with a textbook called *The Fundamentals of Basketball*.

Her efforts paid off. She was invited to play in the World University Games in the Soviet Union in 1973, and then she was chosen as one of twelve players for Team USA to compete in the Olympic Games in Montreal in 1976, where she won a silver medal despite having blown out her ACL just two years before.

In the meantime, she also finished her time at UT Martin, and the university's main campus in Knoxville invited her to come be an assistant coach for their women's basketball team. Before she even had time to respond to the offer, the head coach, Margaret Hutson, left the position. And so Pat, directly out of college, accepted her first and only head coaching job at the University of Tennessee.

She started at UT in 1974, two years before James Cape would sit down to write his letter, and right away she ran into problems with Tennessee high schools' lingering attachment to the half-court game. She needed to fill a competitive collegiate roster, but the only players arriving to her open tryouts were kids from Tennessee—and they'd never been allowed to cross half court.

In 1975, she faced the same obstacle. That year her starting center, Jane Pemberton, came in having played guard in high school. That meant she had never shot the basketball in an organized game in her life.

The year 1976 started to bring some changes. Most importantly, Title IX led to a massive uptick in financial support from the university. The women's athletics department funding jumped from $5,000 for six sports to $126,000 for seven sports in the span of just one year.

Nevertheless, despite the flashy new budget and the Lady Vols' growing reputation in the community, the program was still hamstrung by the half-court rule in Tennessee high schools. The persistence of the alien form of the game meant that Pat either had to engage in expensive out-of-state recruiting for each and every player, or accept that parts of her roster would be cobbled together from students who had only ever learned half of their sport.

The rule haunted Pat, but it turned out to be one of the few fights in her young life she wouldn't be able to power through on sheer force of will alone. She would need an assist from the mild-mannered Victoria Cape, and the opportunity she was about to provide for Pat to make her case.

5

THE LAWYERS

In October 1974, just as Victoria Cape was starting her basketball career, two recent graduates of the University of Tennessee Law School created their own law firm in their hometown of Oak Ridge. Both of them happened to be women. They didn't set out on their own to make a statement or to advance the cause of women in the legal profession; they did it because they had to. They did it because despite their stellar academic records and achievements, neither received a job offer from any law firm in Knoxville, Oak Ridge, or anywhere else in East Tennessee.

This was the typical lot of women graduating from law school in Tennessee in the mid 1970s. Law firms were male bastions. If a young woman got an interview with a hiring partner at one of those firms, the best she could generally hope for was an offer to become a legal secretary. And so Ann Mostoller and Dorothy Stulberg hung out their shingle as the new firm of Mostoller & Stulberg in the Cappiello Building on Tulsa Avenue in Oak Ridge.

Their first victory came when, to their surprise, the Bank of Oak Ridge lent them $2,000 in start-up money without requiring their husbands' signatures. In those days, such a loan to a young businesswoman was about as rare as a job offer from an established law firm.

Most new lawyers fresh from passing the bar examination have little real-world experience to bring to their infant practice. But Ann Mostoller and Dorothy Stulberg were not your typical new lawyers, even apart from their gender.

Mostoller was a graduate of Brown University and had been an active member of the American Civil Liberties Union and the National Organization for Women even before she decided to attend law school. She had also established a family. Her husband, Mark Mostoller, worked for the Oak Ridge National Laboratory, and she and Mark had two children, Katy and Quenton. Both were preschoolers when Ann started law school, making her the prototypical working mom long before the role became a mainstream phenomenon.

Dorothy Stulberg had a similar background as an educated working mother and activist in the Oak Ridge community. She got her bachelor's degree from Iowa State

University and a master's degree from the University of Minnesota. Her husband Mel worked in the Biology Division of the Oak Ridge National Laboratory, and the Stulbergs had three daughters—Laurie, Lisa, and Lynn—whom Dorothy drove to school each morning before she made the forty-minute trek to Knoxville to attend her law school classes.

As if being a law student, a wife, and the mother of three small children wasn't enough for one resume, Dorothy had also long been a leader in the Oak Ridge League of Women Voters and a community activist. She once succinctly stated her decision to pursue a legal career: "The reason I became a lawyer is because so many people are considered less than valuable. I believe in the value of human beings."

Ann Mostoller and Dorothy Stulberg had actually started practicing law before they ever got that two thousand-dollar loan from the Bank of Oak Ridge that enabled them to open the offices of Mostoller & Stulberg. As law students, both were active in the University of Tennessee Legal Clinic, and under the supervision of law professors, they actually represented indigent clients in court proceedings in Knoxville and Oak Ridge.

When the new firm of Mostoller & Stulberg opened in Oak Ridge in the fall of 1974 it was, in effect, a working legal clinic. Both Ann and Dorothy advised local judges that they would happily accept appointments to criminal cases. Within a year, both were appointed to serve as public defenders in Anderson County and were plunged into criminal jury trials, an almost unheard of experience for a young lawyer right out of law school. "They call it law practice," Ann Mostoller recalls, laughing. "But in the case of Dorothy and me, we were truly 'practicing.'"

They also began to build a divorce practice, serving low-income clients by offering divorce counsel at fees based on incomes. And on top of *that*, they established an office practice, drafting wills and counseling folks from Oak Ridge on numerous legal matters. Again, such a practice was unusual for brand new lawyers, but Ann and Dorothy brought with them a long history of their leadership in the Oak Ridge community. Many of their clients were their fellow community activists.

And one of those clients was James Cape.

Dorothy Stulberg and Jim, as she called him, had been friends long before Dorothy went to law school. They played bridge together and worked together in the League of Women Voters and on projects for the Community Action Commission.

While Jim Cape was a scientist, he was also an accomplished businessman who invested in real estate, owning both commercial and residential rental property across Oak Ridge. He needed a lawyer, so when the law office of Mostoller & Stulberg opened its doors, he was one of the first clients to walk in.

Jim Cape also had something in common with his old friend Dorothy Stulberg: he was the father of a daughter he adored. Victoria Cape was the same age as Dorothy's daughter, Lisa, and close in age to Laurie and Lynn Stulberg. Dorothy and Jim often compared notes about parenting as they played bridge or sat beside each other at local political gatherings.

It was during one of those conversations in the winter of 1976 that Jim Cape shared with Dorothy his frustration over Victoria's participation on the Oak Ridge High School girls' basketball team — or more accurately, the limits of her participation. Jim told Dorothy that while Victoria was one of the best rebounders on the team, she was only allowed to make a defensive rebound and was then not allowed to dribble or pass the ball past the half-court line, and was never allowed to shoot the ball.

Women's basketball was another developing mutual interest of Jim and Dorothy. They were both fans of the Lady Vols, the women's basketball team at the University of Tennessee that was starting to establish a following thanks to a dynamic young head coach named Pat Head. Jim and the Stulbergs often attended Lady Vols games together at the old Alumni Gym on the UT campus, cheering on young women as they raced up and down the court.

Jim made no secret about the fact that he dreamed that Victoria might someday play college basketball herself, just as he had played the game at the University of Michigan. But he saw no prospect of Victoria ever playing college ball if she wasn't even allowed to shoot the ball in high school.

At some point, Ann Mostoller was brought into the conversation. She recalled playing girls' high school basketball in Pittsburgh where she grew up. Ann shook her head and said, "Not only were we confined to the split-court game; there was also a 'two-dribble' rule. We were only allowed to take two dribbles before we had to pass the ball!"

Jim told Dorothy and Ann that he had written to the TSSAA expressing his strong opinion that the rules should be changed to allow Victoria and other girls across Tennessee to play full court. He told them he had received a response from the TSSAA, but to his disappointment, it had been basically, "Thank you for your letter, but we are not going to change the game."

Jim regarded it as sex discrimination. Dorothy and Ann both agreed, and began to make plans to launch a full-court press on behalf of Victoria, her teammates at Oak Ridge High School, and young female basketball players across the Volunteer State.

Approximately two hundred miles west of Oak Ridge, Charles Hampton White worked in his law office in downtown Nashville, a partner in the well-established law firm of Cornelius, Collins & White. Charles Hampton White was the classic southern lawyer. He was also a classic officer and a gentleman.

An honors graduate of Vanderbilt University, Charles served as an officer in the United States Navy. Upon his discharge, he enrolled at Harvard Law School, where he excelled just as he had as an undergraduate at Vanderbilt.

In 1955, upon his graduation from Harvard, he returned to his hometown of Nashville, where he established a very successful law practice and became accomplished as a trial lawyer.

He enjoyed law practice, but he was also a multi-dimensional man who loved the arts, particularly opera. He read voraciously, was a member of the educational charity the English Speaking Union, and enjoyed traveling with his family.

Charles became one of the most respected members of the Nashville Bar, known for his quiet but effective advocacy style in the courtroom and for his role as counselor to numerous Nashville businesses, particularly in the area of labor relations. And along the way, he also developed a unique reputation. He became known as "the teachers' lawyer." He had enormous respect for educators, and felt honored to be their voice.

While he was not an athlete, Charles had particular regard for teachers who were coaches. He saw interscholastic athletics not as an end in itself, but as a wonderful teaching tool for young men. He truly believed that if you excelled in both the classroom and on a football gridiron, a basketball court, a baseball diamond, or a running track, you were going to excel in all aspects of life. So beginning in the late 1950s, Charles Hampton White and his firm began to represent the Tennessee Education Association and the TSSAA.

He enjoyed the work. He met frequently with Tennessee high school athletic directors and coaches, counseling them on how to effectively run their programs. He also represented the TSSAA in numerous cases over the years, including a long TSSAA legal battle involving private schools in Tennessee that offered athletic scholarships, to the frustration of public school coaches who saw themselves losing some of their best players in the process. As a "teachers' lawyer," Charles no doubt saw his representation of the TSSAA as a chance to enhance educational opportunities for student athletes in Tennessee schools.

In the spring of 1976, Charles Hampton White got a phone call from Gil Gideon, the executive secretary of the TSSAA. Gideon informed his lawyer that he had received a series of letters from a young lady named Victoria Cape. She said she was a member of the girls' basketball team at Oak Ridge High School and expressed her displeasure with the split-court game the TSSAA imposed on her and her teammates. She requested the TSSAA change the rule so that she and girls' basketball players across the state could play full court.

Charles Hampton White reviewed the letters. On June 2, 1976, he sent Victoria Cape a response. It was simple and to the point: "TSSAA has no present intention to change the half-court six-girl basketball rule for the 1976–77 school year."

A little over two months later, Counselor White received another phone call from Gil Gideon.

Victoria Cape had filed a lawsuit.

6

THE LAWSUIT

On the morning of August 18, 1976, Ann Mostoller drove to the federal courthouse in Knoxville, entered the clerk's office, and filed a lawsuit on behalf of Victoria Ann Cape.

Since Victoria was a minor, the suit was filed "by and through James Cape, father and next friend."

The named defendants were the TSSAA, the Board of Education of Oak Ridge, Tennessee, and Kenneth L. Loflin, superintendent of schools for Oak Ridge. The lawsuit also named as defendants Billy Williams, the Oak Ridge Schools athletic director, and Sudartha Vann, head basketball coach of the Oak Ridge High School girls' team.

Victoria was mildly embarrassed that she had sued her coach and her school, but Ann and Dorothy explained to her that they were necessary defendants. Moreover, the lawsuit was not a surprise to Athletic Director Williams, Coach Vann, or Superintendent Loflin. They knew it was coming.

The lawsuit was filed pursuant to Title IX, the Fourteenth Amendment to the Constitution of the United States, and 42 U.S.C. §1983, a provision of the Civil Rights Act of 1871 that allows for lawsuits against public officials for violations of constitutional rights. It noted that the TSSAA was a voluntary association of public secondary schools in Tennessee whose members were tax-supported public institutions that held sporting events in facilities constructed, operated, and maintained at taxpayer expense. The individual defendants were all officials at Oak Ridge High School, a public school.

The lawsuit charged that the defendants, acting "under color of state law," had adopted and were enforcing a rule promulgated by the TSSAA which stated that female student basketball players had to play the game of basketball by rules different from those used by male high school players. The Complaint noted that the stated reason for the different rules were "to keep girls' games from being as strenuous as boys' games," and it went on to briefly describe the main components of the TSSAA rules for girls' basketball, providing "that each player plays only one-half of the entire basketball court, and each player plays only guard or forward."

.

The Complaint further noted that Victoria Cape had written numerous letters to the executive secretary of the TSSAA "to express her displeasure with the format for girls' basketball and to urge the adoption of the rules presently utilized in boys' basketball, including five players in use of the full court." Attached as an exhibit to the Complaint was Charles Hampton White's letter to Ms. Cape, dated June 2, 1976, in which he advised that the TSSAA had no intention to change the half-court, six-girl basketball rule.

The heart of the Complaint then came in the sixth paragraph. Victoria Cape alleged that she was "being denied the full pleasure of the game of basketball." She noted that in her position as guard, "she is never able to 'set up plays' and participate in the full planning and strategy of the game." The Complaint further contended that Victoria was "also denied the continuous action and consequent physical development that results from playing the full court game," and that "her future as a basketball player [would] be seriously hampered by the continuous use of the 'girls' rules of basketball."

While young Victoria privately doubted she could fulfill her father's dream of her playing college basketball, her Complaint urged that dream could never be realized so long as Victoria was confined to half a basketball court. As proof, a copy of a letter to Victoria Cape from Barbara Abernathy, director of women's athletics at Southern

Connecticut State College, was attached as Exhibit 2. Coach Abernathy said in her letter that Victoria would "likely not be considered as worth recruiting and would definitely not have any edge at all if an athletic scholarship based on basketball ability were concerned."

Finally, the Complaint averred that there were "no physical attributes of women which prevent them from utilizing the entire basketball court; that, in fact, this is the only way to utilize and train the body completely."

The Complaint concluded with what lawyers call the "prayer for relief." Victoria Cape asked the Court to issue both a temporary and permanent injunction "requiring defendants to adopt the five-on-five, full-court basketball rules for the girls' athletics program that are presently in use in the boys' athletics program in the public high schools in the State of Tennessee for the 1976 basketball season."

Victoria also requested a specific finding by the Court "that the enforcement of the limited 'girls' rules for secondary school basketball" was "an arbitrary and capricious and an unreasonable rule based on an anachronism and acts to deprive [Victoria] of future financial scholarship assistance and other financial gain, and also is in violation of [her] constitutional and civil rights." The legal language of the Complaint may have been complicated, but its intention was clear: the half-court game was outdated, unfair, and detrimental to the hopes and ambitions of young women who wanted to compete on the same level as men.

And so finally, the Complaint requested compensatory and punitive damages in the amount of $5,000 and reasonable attorney's fees.

The Complaint was stamped "filed" in the Federal Court Clerk's Office, and the case was assigned to Judge Robert Taylor, himself a former college basketball player.

THE JUDGE

Judge Robert Love Taylor was a product of one of the most colorful families in Tennessee history. The Taylors loved politics, law, music, and literature, and as orators, musicians, and poets, they had a profound impact on the Volunteer State in each.

Judge Taylor's father, Alfred, served as governor of Tennessee. Judge Taylor's uncle, Robert Taylor (after whom Judge Taylor was named), also served as governor. In 1886, they both ran for governor of Tennessee, against one another. Alfred, or Alf as he was better known, ran on the Republican ticket, while Bob ran on the Democratic ticket. There was even a *third* Taylor in the race. Alf and Bob's father, Nathaniel, was the candidate of the Prohibition ticket, although he did not actively campaign.

Unsurprisingly, a race this offbeat attracted national attention, becoming known not only in Tennessee but also throughout America as "The War of the Roses," named for the famous fifteenth-century battle for the throne of England. Newspapers across the country featured lithographs of the Taylor brothers campaigning against each other, side by side, Bob wearing a white rose and Alf a red one. For three months, Alf and Bob traveled together across Tennessee, sleeping in the same bed, eating at the same table.

They appeared in courthouse squares and at gatherings, debating each other and playing their fiddles to the delight of thousands. "We are two roses from the same garden," Bob declared. And as they ran vigorously against each other, they seemed to have as much fun as the crowds they entertained.

In his last speech of their final debate at the end of the campaign, Alf said, "I say to you now, that after all these eventful struggles, I still love my brother of old, with an undying affection—but politically, my friends, I despise him!"

Bob won the election by thirteen thousand votes, served three terms as governor, and was eventually elected to the United States Senate in 1907. In Washington, he regaled President William Howard Taft and his fellow senators with Tennessee stories and came to be known as "the most popular man in the United States Senate." Afterwards, Alf also went to Washington, serving three terms in the US House of Representatives. Then, in his 70s, he was finally elected governor in his own right.

Along the way, the Taylor brothers continued to entertain the folks of Tennessee, and not just during elections. They created their own two-man vaudeville show of sorts called "Yankee Doodle and Dixie" that featured them fiddling, singing, and lecturing.

The family's talents also extended to the written word. Governor Bob Taylor's grandson, Peter Taylor, was a Pulitzer Prize–winning author who wrote about his remarkable family in such works as *In the Tennessee County* and *A Summons to Memphis*.

It was into this extraordinary family that Robert Love Taylor was born in 1899, the seventh of ten children. He was destined from the start to carry on the family tradition of law and politics, but he would also pursue a unique interest of his own: sports.

As a boy, he loved baseball and excelled in it. During the summers of his undergraduate years at Milligan College, he played semi-pro baseball and no doubt dreamed about being a big leaguer. But rather than pursuing professional baseball, he pursued the legal profession, studying law at Vanderbilt in 1922 and 1923, and finishing his legal education at Yale in 1924. Though his dreams of playing Major League Baseball may have died, his love for the national pastime never did.

Following his graduation from Yale, Robert Taylor immersed himself in law, and ultimately politics. While he never entertained crowds in courthouse squares playing the fiddle like his father and uncle, he entertained courthouse crowds in East Tennessee serving as a colorful counsel in jury trials.

As his fame spread through the courthouses, he was urged to get into politics and even become the latest member of the Taylor family to run for governor. In 1948, he became chairman of the Tennessee State Democratic Executive Committee, casting his political lot with his Uncle Bob's party rather than his father's GOP.

As Democratic state party chair, he managed the successful election of Gordon Browning as governor. That same year, he shaped Tennessee political history when he successfully managed the campaign of Estes Kefauver for the United States Senate. Kefauver would become a maverick figure in the Senate, leading nationally televised committee hearings on organized crime, running for president three times, and winning the Democratic Party's nomination for vice president in 1956. That same year, Kefauver was one of only three southern senators who refused to sign the "Southern Manifesto" in which southern congressmen vowed to oppose the US Supreme Court's decision in *Brown v. Board of Education*.

Judge Taylor's role in the election of Senator Kefauver made him a leading figure in national Democratic politics and caught the attention of President of Harry S. Truman. In 1949, President Truman nominated him for the vacant federal judgeship in the Eastern District of Tennessee, and his appointment was confirmed in the US Senate in March 1950.

Upon assuming the federal bench, Judge Taylor quickly developed a reputation as a workaholic who never took a vacation or even a day off. He disregarded federal holidays, dismissing them as "congressional holidays."

His docket became the most current in the entire federal judicial system. Even in the 1950s, it would often take a year or more for a case to come to trial after it was filed. But with Judge Taylor, a scant three months or less generally elapsed between the time a case was filed and the time it was tried. In fact, Judge Taylor was sometimes known to set a case for trial within days after it was filed, even before the defendant had submitted an answer.

He also became known as a flamboyant figure in his courtroom as he presided over trials. Most judges sit quietly on the bench as hearings or trials proceed, patiently listening to the lawyers and witnesses, and speaking only to make rulings on objections or to ultimately render a decision. But lawyers who appeared in Judge Taylor's courtroom quickly learned that he had no hesitation to interject himself into a case. He would interrupt a lawyer's examination of a witness by asking questions himself. When he heard witnesses' answers, he often commented on them, to the intense disconsolation of counsel.

"He could take over a case from you," recalled one trial lawyer. "If he were on your side, it was great. But when he was against you, it was really difficult. It's hard enough fighting another lawyer, but you simply can't fight the judge."

Following the landmark decision of the US Supreme Court in *Brown v. Board of Education*, Judge Taylor handled the south's first school desegregation case. With more than all deliberate speed, the judge ordered the Anderson County, Tennessee School System to admit black students to the previously all-white Clinton High School.

In the years to follow, Judge Taylor developed a friendship with US Chief Justice Warren Burger. Chief Justice Burger called upon Judge Taylor to preside over high-profile cases in other jurisdictions. Two of those cases were public corruption trials of governors, Maryland Governor Marvin Mandel on charges of mail fraud and racketeering, and US Court of Appeals Judge Otto Kerner, who was charged with bribery, conspiracy, mail fraud, perjury, and tax evasion for actions allegedly taken while serving as governor of Illinois. It was the first time in history that a federal appellate judge had been tried on criminal charges.

Judge Taylor confided to associates that he was not entirely comfortable trying cases against governors since, as the son of a governor, he knew firsthand the pressures placed on a state's chief executive. But Judge Taylor did his duty, sentencing both Judge Kerner and Governor Mandel to years in prison following their convictions by juries.

During his years on the bench, Judge Taylor maintained his love of and interest in baseball. During his frequent in-court comments, he often stated, "Watching good lawyers at work in the courtroom is like watching a good infield at play." While he never took a day off, he would leave the bench on October afternoons when the World Series was being played so he could watch the games on TV in his chambers.

His love of baseball became so well known to lawyers who appeared in his courtroom that they were always trying to come up with baseball analogies to use during arguments before him. Charles Susano, who later became an appellate judge himself, recalls that as a young lawyer appearing before Judge Taylor, he would invariably say something like, "Your Honor, this case is just like baseball." And he would then try to persuade Judge Taylor that his client had made a legal hit or even a home run, while his adversary had committed an error.

Judge Taylor clearly loved applying baseball to the law, which may explain why he would enjoy the chance to turn around and apply the law to another sport: basketball.

Each year graduates at the top of their law school classes are offered judicial clerkships with federal judges like Robert Taylor. The judicial law clerks review each case assigned to a judge, extensively research the law underlying the case, and often assist the judge in writing the case decisions. It is the plum job for a new lawyer and often the first step toward someday becoming a federal judge in their own right. Indeed, most US Supreme Court justices began their careers as law clerks.

In the spring of 1976, young Charles Huddleston graduated with highest honors from the University of Tennessee College of Law and was offered and accepted a position as one of Judge Taylor's law clerks. Unlike Judge Taylor, Charles was the first in his family to enter the ring of politics and law. But like the judge, he had strong ties to the world of athletics. In fact, Charles was a member of one of the leading families in Tennessee sports — the Majors family. Charles's mother was the first cousin of the legendary Johnny Majors, an All-American football player who would become one of the most successful head football coaches in University of Tennessee history. Charles's mother had been a Majors athlete herself, playing tennis at Tennessee Tech. His father had also been a college athlete, and later a girls' high school basketball coach, so Charles had literally grown up in gymnasiums. Before deciding to attend law school, he had often dreamed of becoming a basketball coach himself. And even though he ultimately chose law school, he never lost his love of sports, particularly basketball.

Because his mother was a college athlete and his father had coached female players, Charles had a particular interest in women's basketball. On winter nights he would often leave the law school library to take a break from his studies and watch the University of Tennessee Lady Vols play basketball in Alumni Gym. He loved watching them play and was always intrigued by the fact that they played full court rather than the split-court game his father had coached. While he was excited about his new career in law, Charles never forgot his first dream of being a teacher and a coach, and he often thought about that as he sat in Alumni Gym watching the Lady Vols.

As Judge Taylor's law clerk, Charles reviewed the initial paperwork for each new matter filed in the United States District Court for the Eastern District of Tennessee. There were criminal indictments, petitions, and civil complaints, and after a while, one legal pleading pretty much started to look like the next.

And then one morning, Charles reviewed a pleading that was far from routine. It was a lawsuit about basketball, the game he had loved his entire life. And it wasn't just about basketball—it was about women's basketball.

Charles was intrigued. Here was a lawsuit that brought together the two loves of his—and Judge Taylor's—life: sports and the law.

Victoria Cape, Oak Ridge Wildcat, 1976. Courtesy of Victoria Hermes.

Victoria Cape (no. 42) matching an attacking ballhandler stride for stride. Courtesy of Victoria Hermes.

Victoria Cape awaits a rebound. Courtesy of Victoria Hermes.

James Cape, ca. 1980. Cape moved his family to Oak Ridge, Tennessee, to take a job at Oak Ridge National Laboratory. An athlete himself, he was astounded when, after encouraging his daughter Victoria to try out for her high school basketball team, he discovered girls in Tennessee played a very different game than boys. He encouraged her to file the lawsuit. Courtesy of Victoria Hermes.

Ann Mosteller and Dorothy Stulberg founded their own law firm in Oak Ridge in 1974. They provided excellent representation for Victoria Cape as she pursued her lawsuit. Courtesy of the *Oak Ridger*.

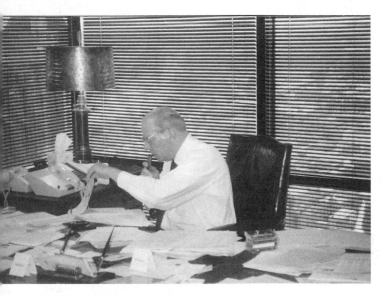

Charles Hampton White, a gentlemanly lawyer in a well-established law firm in Nashville, represented the Tennessee Secondary School Athletic Association (TSSAA) as it fought Victoria Cape's lawsuit. This picture was taken around 1994. Courtesy of Cornelius and Collins, LLP.

Charles Huddleston, Judge Robert Taylor's law clerk at the time the judge heard *Victoria Cape v. TSSAA*. Courtesy of the Historical Society of the United States District Court for the Eastern District of Tennessee, Inc.

A product of one of the most colorful families in Tennessee, Robert Love Taylor presided over *Victoria Cape v. TSSAA*. Courtesy of the Historical Society of the United States District Court for the Eastern District of Tennessee, Inc.

The Eastern District Courthouse at about the time of the trial.
Courtesy of the Historical Society of the United States
District Court for the Eastern District of Tennessee, Inc.

Pat Summitt played a crucial role in *Victoria Cape v. TSSAA*, even as she was beginning her illustrious career as the winningest college basketball coach in NCAA history. Just a few short years before, she had been a star player at University of Tennessee at Martin. Courtesy of UT Martin Chancellor Keith Carver.

Coach Pat (Head) Summitt consults with Assistant Coach
Mickie DeMoss at a Lady Vols basketball game in the early
1980s, just a few years after the events recounted in this book.
Courtesy of University of Tennessee, Knoxville, Athletics
Department Archives.

Ann Mostoller in 2012. Courtesy of Mostoller, Stulberg, Whitfield & Allen.

Victoria (Cape) Hermes in 2018. Courtesy of Victoria Hermes.

8

THE TRIAL BEGINS

Lawsuits in American courts often proceed at a glacial pace. It is not uncommon for years to elapse between the time a case is filed and when it ultimately resolved in a trial. But in Judge Robert Taylor's courtroom, the duration of a case was not measured in years and hardly even in months. It would often be just a matter of weeks that would transpire between the time a case was filed and the time it would be tried by an anxious and efficient Judge Taylor. In the case of *Victoria Cape v. TSSAA*, it appeared at the outset that the case would be resolved in a matter of days.

Hours after Ann Mostoller filed the lawsuit on August 13, 1976, Judge Taylor entered an order setting the matter for hearing a breathtaking six days later, on August 19. The order stated that the defendants would appear and "show cause" why the Court should not grant the relief Victoria Cape sought in her Complaint.

The setting of the case for a show cause hearing less than a week after it was filed proved to be unworkable for the simple reason not all of the defendants were served with a copy of the Complaint by August 19. This resulted in a five-day continuance of the hearing to August 24, 1976, by which time all the defendants had been served, and, at least from Judge Taylor's perspective, had ample time to prepare their defense to Victoria Cape's case.

At 9:55 a.m. on August 24, 1976, Judge Taylor entered his courtroom and took his seat on the bench. Ann Mostoller rose from the counsel table, as did Victoria Cape behind her, and Charles Hampton White across from her at the defense counsel table. He was joined by Phillip Condra of Oak Ridge, who represented the Oak Ridge School Board, Superintendent Loflin, Athletic Director Williams, and Coach Vann.

Condra, a bright young lawyer, had the perfect resume to join Charles Hampton White as defense counsel in this particular case. He had played football and baseball at Sewanee, where he graduated Phi Beta Kappa. Before attending law school, he coached football, baseball, and wrestling at Montgomery Bell Academy, a boys' prep school in Nashville.

The clerk called the court to order and then announced, "Civil Action 3–76–234, Victoria Ann Cape versus Tennessee Secondary School Athletic Association." It was technically not a trial, but a hearing—although in substance, it was indeed a trial. There was no jury; it was what lawyers call a "bench trial," with the decision in the case being made in effect by a jury of one: Judge Taylor.

As Ann Mostoller rose to make an opening statement, she recalled with some bemusement her first appearance before Judge Taylor some two years earlier when she and her partner Dorothy Stulberg had just passed the Tennessee Bar Exam and were admitted as lawyers of the United States District Court for the Eastern District of Tennessee. Upon their introduction, an apparently bewildered Judge Taylor said to them, "I don't know what to call you ladies!"

It was not the first time Judge Taylor had greeted female attorneys in such a manner. On one occasion, he addressed a female prosecutor as "Mr. Lady Prosecutor."

After Dorothy Stulberg had made a few more court appearances, invariably representing indigent clients, Judge Taylor began to address her as "Social Worker Stulberg." Dorothy Stulberg was not sure it was meant as a compliment, but she took it as one.

But on the morning of August 24, 1976, Judge Taylor did not address "Lady Mostoller" at all. He simply looked at counsel and asked, "All right, who is to be heard?" Ann Mostoller then announced that she was "one of the attorneys for Miss Cape," and that she and Charles Hampton White had reached a number of stipulations.

Judge Taylor loved stipulations—the more the better. He wanted to get down to business in all of his trials and hear evidence and argument only about the contested issues before the Court.

Ann Mostoller knew this, so she quickly announced that she and Mr. White had agreed that Oak Ridge High School was a public school and a member of the TSSAA. She further announced that it was agreed that Oak Ridge High School received state and federal funding, that Vickie Cape was a student at Oak Ridge High School, and that she played for the girls' basketball team under rules set by the TSSAA. Finally, Ann Mostoller announced that the rules the TSSAA set for girls' basketball were different from the rules set for boys' basketball.

With that, she made no further opening statement. She advised the Court that she was ready to call her first witness, Victoria Cape.

A clearly nervous, young Victoria took the stand and was administered the oath. As the soft-spoken Victoria began to answer her counsel's questions, Judge Taylor could not hear her. He leaned toward her from the bench and admonished her, "Now a basketball player should talk louder than that."

He then gave her some advice: "[You] can scream at the referee, talk like that."

Victoria could not recall ever yelling at a ref, but she did try to raise her voice in the courtroom.

Ann Mostoller began to lead Victoria through her testimony. Victoria told the Court that she was about to start her junior year at Oak Ridge High School, where she was a member of the basketball team. She testified that she played guard and explained to the Court that under the rules as set by the TSSAA, she could never shoot the ball, set up plays, or dribble the ball past half court.

At that point, Judge Taylor interrupted and took over the examination of Victoria Cape himself, eliciting the following testimony:

JUDGE TAYLOR:

What if the guard shoots under the rules you play under now? What happens?

VICTORIA:

You can't.

JUDGE TAYLOR:

What does the referee do?

VICTORIA:

I wouldn't know. Nobody has ever done it.

JUDGE TAYLOR:

Is a foul across [*sic*] the line?

VICTORIA:

No, it isn't a foul, it's just a rule that you cannot and if you do the other team takes the ball.

JUDGE TAYLOR:

You lose the ball if the guard crosses the line?

VICTORIA:

That's right.

JUDGE TAYLOR:

> That's a pretty big penalty, isn't it? You want the ball, don't you, your team?

VICTORIA:

> Yes.

JUDGE TAYLOR:

> You can't make a goal unless you have the ball, can you?

VICTORIA:

> That's true.

Ann Mostoller was more than happy to let Judge Taylor take over the examination of Victoria. Judge Taylor seemed to be enjoying himself, and he was clearly showing sympathy to Victoria's plight, given the restrictions placed on her as a basketball player.

After Judge Taylor finished his line of questioning, Ann Mostoller resumed her examination of Victoria, asking her about her experience playing full-court basketball. Victoria told the Court that during the previous summer, she had attended basketball camps at the University of Tennessee and at Maryville College, where she played the position of center in a five-player, full-court game.

Charles Hampton White rose at this point and objected, contending that Victoria Cape's summer camp basketball experience was irrelevant to the issues in the case.

Judge Taylor did not even wait for a response from Ann Mostoller. He immediately overruled the objection, saying, "Well, it might show her potentiality if she gets to a university where she can play the entire court."

Charles Hampton White responded, "I would submit, your honor, she is not going to get a scholarship based on summer camp activities."

Judge Taylor replied, "She might, might not, depending upon how well she plays in summer camp, I would say."

After Mr. White's objection was overruled, Ann Mostoller asked Victoria about her experience playing full-court basketball at the summer camps. She responded that it was more tiring than playing the half-court game, but she enjoyed it and could do it.

Mostoller then asked Victoria about her dreams of playing basketball beyond high school. Victoria made no claim of being a superstar basketball player or a top college prospect, but she said she did hope to play basketball in college, perhaps even with a scholarship. She expressed concern that having never been allowed to play full court except at summer basketball camp, she would not have the opportunity to play the college game.

At this point, Judge Taylor again interrupted and resumed his own examination of Victoria:

JUDGE TAYLOR:
Now do these colleges and universities give scholarships to girls that play basketball?

VICTORIA:
Yes, they do.

JUDGE TAYLOR:

The university over here gives them?

VICTORIA:

UT?

JUDGE TAYLOR:

Yes.

VICTORIA:

I believe, yes.

JUDGE TAYLOR:

Does Maryville give one?

VICTORIA:

I really don't know.

JUDGE TAYLOR:

Carson-Newman?

VICTORIA:

I don't know.

JUDGE TAYLOR:

Tusculum?

VICTORIA:

I don't know.

JUDGE TAYLOR:

Milligan?

VICTORIA:

Never heard of them.

JUDGE TAYLOR:

Never heard of Milligan? Good gracious.

At this point there was laughter in the courtroom, coming from the clerk, the court reporter, Judge Taylor's law clerk, and others present who knew that Judge Taylor had once played college basketball at Milligan.

Judge Taylor smiled and led the laughter.

At this point Ann Mostoller announced that she had no further questions for Ms. Cape. She had established the three points she wanted to convey through Victoria's testimony: first, that Victoria played the TSSAA-imposed, restricted version of basketball as a guard on her high school team. Second, that she was capable of playing the five-player, full-court game given that she had played it as a center at summer basketball camps. And third, that she wanted the opportunity to play women's college basketball but was concerned she might never get the chance given the limited role she played in the high school game.

Charles Hampton White then began his cross-examination of Victoria. He faced the challenge lawyers always face when cross-examining a minor: he had to be courteous to young Victoria and not risk offending Judge Taylor, who had smiled at Victoria throughout her testimony. But at the same time, he had to elicit from her the information he needed to defend his client.

Charles Hampton White did it skillfully, gently getting Victoria to admit that she had tried out for the position of guard on the team, not forward, and knew that in that position she would not be able to set up plays, shoot the ball, or dribble the ball past half court. He further got Victoria to admit that her coach, defendant Sudartha Vann, was the person who decided which position a member of the team should play, and that Coach Vann had no doubt made her decision regarding Victoria based on Victoria's skill and ability in handling or shooting the ball. Finally, White got Victoria to acknowledge that her team played in the same gym as did the boys' team, wore uniforms "just like the boys," and had a paid coach who was a member of the faculty, just like the boys team did.

Charles Hampton White sat down, and a relieved Victoria Cape stood up to leave the witness box. Judge Taylor told her to remain seated, and he resumed his questioning of her.

"Why do you want this court to issue an Order against the School Board, against this other defendant, Tennessee Secondary School Athletic Association, to permit you to play on a full court rather than a half court; why do you want that? . . . What good is it going to do you to get an Order of that kind?"

Victoria responded, "Well, girls from all over Tennessee can, you know, play, get to play full court, and when they go to college they have more of a chance of getting a scholarship, and it just doesn't seem right to play half court."

"Are you working toward a scholarship?" asked Judge Taylor.

"I would like," said Victoria, "if I am able to play full court."

Judge Taylor then asked her whether her coach had ever told her she had the potential to reach of her goal of being a university or college player.

Victoria honestly responded, "I don't know. She has never said nothing." Judge Taylor then asked her, "How do you know that you would ever have a chance to make the [college] teams?"

Again, Victoria modestly replied, "I don't . . . but I'm going to try."

Finally, Judge Taylor asked Victoria about her experience playing full court at summer basketball camps. "How did you get along with playing under the boys' rules?" he asked.

Again Victoria candidly responded, "It got me tired, but I just kept on going. I didn't give out."

At this point, Judge Taylor asked if either side wanted to examine Victoria further. All counsel responded they had no further questions for her.

Ann Mostoller then called her second witness, Jackie Butler, the head basketball coach at Harriman High School in nearby Harriman, Tennessee.

Coach Butler testified that during her school days, she had played three different forms of girls' basketball. In junior high and high school in Kingston, Tennessee, she had played the split-court, six-player game. She then attended Hiwassee Junior College, where she played the split-court game, but with one player as a "rover" who could run the full court. She completed her athletic career at East

Tennessee State University, where she played the full-court, five-player game, "like the boys."

Coach Butler testified that Tennessee high school girls were capable of playing full-court basketball, but flatly stated that the reason they were not allowed to do so was because "there are too many men coaching ball" and "too many men setting the rules for girls and women, and we know what we can do and they don't think we can do it."

Ann Mostoller asked her about opportunities for Tennessee girls' high school basketball players to receive athletic scholarships to play the women's game in college. Coach Butler responded that college coaches had told her, "We are interested in your offensive people, [but] we are not interested in your defensive people because we feel like it is much easier to train someone to defend than it is to teach them how to shoot."

Defense counsel objected, apparently on the basis of hearsay, but Judge Taylor promptly overruled the objection.

On cross-examination, Phillip Condra got Coach Butler to admit that she made the basketball team at East Tennessee State University and played the full-court game despite the fact that she had been confined to the split-court game in high school.

Condra asked Coach Butler whether she received an athletic scholarship to East Tennessee State.

Coach Butler replied that East Tennessee State didn't give basketball scholarships to women when she played.

Judge Taylor interrupted with one word: "Stingy."

Coach Butler agreed, saying, "That's right."

Finally, Phillip Condra got Coach Butler to acknowledge that college coaches were recruiting Tennessee girls for college basketball "despite the restrictions of the split-court game."

Ann Mostoller then rested, telling the Court, "That is our case, Your Honor."

It was now the defense's turn, and Charles Hampton White announced that the TSSAA would call its first witness, Mr. Gil Gideon, the TSSAA executive secretary.

Gideon testified that the TSSAA set the rules for both boys' and girls' high school basketball in Tennessee, and the rules were "exactly the same" with just a few exceptions. The exceptions were that the girls played with six players to a team, three forwards on one end of the court and three guards on the other. A line that they could not cross divided the court. The guards played defense and could not shoot the ball, while the forwards constituted the "scoring team." The girls played four seven-minute quarters, and the boys played eight. If the game went into overtime, the boys would play for three additional minutes, and the girls for two.

Otherwise the games were exactly the same, and boys' and girls' teams across the state used the same gyms at their high schools.

Gideon praised his split-court, six-person girls' basketball format, saying it was a "more interesting game, and one that our fans understand and appreciate." Gideon also described it as "a wholesome game one [in] which the girls can make use of their physical talents without having to strain themselves in running the full court." He went on to explain that the girls' game had the virtue that it allowed more girls to participate, and it particularly benefitted "the clumsy girl or someone of that sort who cannot play the full court game, and we do have many girls in that respect."

Ann Mostoller than cross-examined Mr. Gideon, focusing on his defense that the rules benefitted "clumsy girls." With mild sarcasm, Mostoller commended the "clumsy girl" rule, and then asked Gideon, "Well, have you offered this game for boys in these schools? Surely there are clumsy boys who can't run the length of the gym who would appreciate being able to play basketball."

Gideon responded, "No ma'am, we have not offered it."

Mostoller would not give the point up, pressing Gideon, "Do you have some reason why the [six-player, split-court] game has not been offered to the boys?"

Gideon responded that no one had requested it be offered for the boys.

Mostoller then followed up, saying, "Surely there are some boys who would be better accommodated by these girls' rules that are in existence now, wouldn't you agree?"

"Could be," Gideon agreed, although he clearly did not take the suggestion seriously.

The defense then offered its own expert, Gaylord Johnson, the girls' basketball coach at Porter High School in Blount County, one of the most successful girls' high school basketball teams in Tennessee at that time.

Coach Johnson testified that three of his four seniors the preceding season had procured college scholarships, and that two of them were guards rather than forwards. This expert testimony was followed by that of another, McGavock High School Coach Doris Rogers, who gave impressive testimony on behalf of the TSSAA. Rogers, a former All-American, had played on a national championship team for Nashville Business College. She had also played for the US team in the Pan American Games and the full-court, five-player game internationally.

Coach Rogers expressed the expert opinion that the six-player, split-court format was "more suitable for high school girls."

But once again, Judge Taylor interrupted the testimony, asking Coach Rogers, "The object of the game is to put the ball in the basket, bucket, isn't it?"

Coach Rogers responded, "Yes, if you are a forward. If you are a guard the object is to keep the other team from scoring and to obtain the ball."

Judge Taylor pressed the issue, asking, "The only way you can get a bucket is to shoot it, isn't it?"

"That is correct," responded Coach Rogers.

"If you cut a person off from shooting, haven't you cut off much of the game?" asked Judge Taylor.

Charles Hampton White did not object to Judge Taylor's question. He knew it would be futile to do so, as Judge Taylor would quickly overrule the objection.

At this point, the TSSAA presented brief testimony from Oak Ridge School Superintendent Kenneth Loflin, who simply testified that the Oak Ridge School funded both the girls' team and the boys' team, paid stipends to their coaches, and gave both teams equal access to the Oak Ridge High School gymnasium for practice and games.

At the conclusion of Loflin's direct testimony, Ann Mostoller announced that she had no questions to ask him.

At this point, both sides asked Judge Taylor for the trial to be in recess until a later date. Charles Hampton White and Phillip Condra planned to file motions to have the case dismissed.

And Ann Mostoller was already reconsidering her announcement to the Court that she had no further proof or testimony to offer. She was thinking that when the Court resumed the trial, she would call one more expert witness, an Olympian and a college basketball coach who had an office just a mile or so away from the federal courthouse.

9

Xs AND Os

For Charles Hampton White, the issue in the case was simple. He succinctly described it to a *Knoxville News Sentinel* reporter: "Is this important to the Constitution that a girl be allowed to shoot a basketball? After all, she made her choice. She went out for guard. And there's no surety that she'll even make the team this year."

A few days after Judge Taylor recessed the trial, Charles Hampton White and Phillip Condra developed a game plan to have Victoria Cape's case dismissed on the basis that she had no constitutional right to shoot a basketball. They both filed motions to dismiss Victoria Cape's lawsuit for "failure to state a claim for which relief can be granted." It's a common motion for defense attorneys to pursue, and it basically says to the Court that even assuming every fact alleged in the Complaint is true, there is still no legal claim or remedy.

In their brief supporting the motion, White and Condra cited federal cases holding that the "participation in interscholastic sports is not a right guaranteed by the due process clause of the 14th Amendment." Moreover, they argued that in the case of Victoria Cape, she was not being denied her "right" to play high school basketball. She was simply "unhappy and dissatisfied in girls' basketball as played in Tennessee."

White and Condra contended that with the exception of a few minor variances, the game Victoria Cape was playing at Oak Ridge High School featured "the same ball, used on the same court with the same skills, dribbling, blocking, and shooting."

Defense counsel then argued, "All things considered, the plaintiff's evidence simply boils down to her unhappiness with the fact that she can't do exactly as boys do when it comes to basketball . . . this disappointment does not rise to the dignity of a substantial federal [constitutional] question."

Defense counsel also argued that Victoria Cape's lawsuit failed to state a claim for which relief could be granted because there was "no evidence before the Court that Victoria Cape will be a member of the Oak Ridge High School girls' basketball team for the 1976–77 season. That judgment and decision is left entirely to the discretion of her coach which is a matter completely beyond the authority and jurisdiction of TSSAA. Even if . . . Coach Sudartha Vann determines that [Victoria Cape] has sufficient skills to make the team, whether Cape plays or not again depends upon the discretion of Coach Vann. If [Victoria Cape] has the shooting ability which she suggests to the Court that she has, we believe it is quite certain Coach Vann would pick her for a forward rather than a guard. [Victoria Cape] herself can remedy her quandary by going out for a forward position which she admittedly did not do."

Finally, White and Condra pointed out to the Court that even if Victoria Cape were an outstanding player with "great potential for a college scholarship and a professional career," this wouldn't "elevate her disappointment to the status of a constitutionally protected right."

The second prong of the defense game plan was a motion to dismiss Victoria's lawsuit on the basis that she had failed to "exhaust administrative remedies" under Title IX. Phillip Condra filed his motion to dismiss on behalf of the school board, Superintendent Loflin, Athletic Director Williams, and Coach Vann. In his brief supporting this motion, Condra cited federal regulations requiring that to pursue a claim under Title IX, one must submit a complaint through the Civil Rights Office of the Department of Health, Education, and Welfare seeking the relief, and exhaust that process before filing a lawsuit in federal court.

Meanwhile, Ann Mostoller and Dorothy Stulberg had a game plan of their own. First, they responded with a well-researched and well-written brief in opposition to the motions to dismiss. They began their brief by arguing that the Fourteenth Amendment to the United States Constitution provides that no state shall deny any person within its jurisdiction the equal protection of the laws. Mostoller and Stulberg further argued that under Title IX of the Education Amendments of 1972, Victoria Cape was guaranteed equal opportunity in educational endeavors.

Mostoller and Stulberg candidly acknowledged to the Court that "the standard of review appropriate in a sex discrimination case is open to debate and is probably in a state of flux at the present time." But, Mostoller and Stulberg argued, there should be no doubt that sex discrimination in interscholastic athletics is illegal and unconstitutional. While Mostoller and Stulberg did not have a plethora of cases to cite involving the treatment of female athletes, they did cite numerous cases legally challenging educational rules or restrictions applying solely to women.

The leading case noted was *Frontiero v. Richardson*, a landmark 1973 decision of the United States Supreme Court. In that case, US Air Force Lieutenant Sharon Frontiero sought the same benefits for her husband as provided to wives of servicemen. One of the attorneys arguing the case before the nation's highest court was future US Supreme Court Justice Ruth Bader Ginsburg. Ruling in Lt. Frontiero's favor, the US Supreme Court stated, "There can no longer be any doubt but that sex-based classifications are subject to close scrutiny by the courts under the Equal Protection Clause."

Mostoller and Stulberg also cited a recent court of appeals decision which stated that "discrimination on the basis of sex can no longer be justified by reliance on outdated images of women as peculiarly delicate and impressionable creatures in need of protection from the rough and tumble of unvarnished humanity."

Mostoller and Stulberg took strong issue with the defense position that participation in interscholastic athletics was simply an extracurricular activity that was not protected by the United States Constitution. They argued that a student's participation in athletics was an integral part of their education impacting their physical and emotional development, their development as leaders, and their ability to gain the respect of their peers and community members. Mostoller and Stulberg pointed out that the fact that colleges offer scholarships to student athletes proved beyond question that athletics is a part of education and was therefore a right, rather than a privilege.

Mostoller and Stulberg submitted further that even assuming that participation in interscholastic athletics was *not* educational, the "privilege/right distinction" was not viable. The issue was "not whether Vickie Cape has a 'right' to play full-court basketball; the issue is whether she was treated differently from boys in an activity provided by the state. Her right is not the right to play full-court basketball. Her right is the right to be treated the same as boys unless there is a rational basis for her being treated differently."

Mostoller and Stuberg continued in their brief that there was no question that the rules the TSSAA imposed on Victoria Cape and all girls playing Tennessee high school basketball were different from the rules imposed on the boys. Thus, the legal burden was on the TSSAA to show that its rule had a "rational relationship to a legitimate state objective."

Mostoller and Stulberg ridiculed the argument that had been advanced by the TSSAA at the previous hearing that the rules imposed for girls' basketball enhanced the opportunity for the "clumsy, awkward" girl to participate in basketball. They noted that the TSSAA did not "provide a different game for the talented, coordinated girl," but more significantly they argued that such a rationale "blatantly demonstrates that the rule is based on a view of women as inferior."

Finally, Mostoller and Stulberg contended that there could be no doubt that the TSSAA rules for girls' basketball posed a serious risk of irreparable harm to Vickie Cape, as she was being denied 1) the opportunity to learn basketball skills that were utilized only in full-court ball, and 2) the development of physical abilities to the extent that she was able to play the game as well as she might. Whether she ultimately could receive a college scholarship or not,

Vickie and her teammates — and indeed every female high school basketball player in Tennessee — was being told that "no matter how good she is, she could never be as good as a boy." Ann Mostoller and Dorothy Stulberg closed the brief with the theme of their case: "The loss which [Victoria Cape] suffers is not simply the loss of a sport season or of an athletic scholarship, but the loss of her fundamental right to be treated as an equal human being."

Having completed and filed their brief in opposition to the motion to dismiss, Ann Mostoller and Dorothy Stulberg turned their attention to the second part of their game plan. They hoped that at the resumption of the trial, they could present to the Court the testimony of a basketball player and coach who had recently returned to Knoxville after winning a silver medal at the Olympic Games.

10

THE NEW EXPERT

On December 7, 1974, twenty-two-year-old Patricia Sue Ann Head led her Lady Vols basketball team onto the court at Alumni Gym, a fifty-year-old building on the University of Tennessee campus that had once been the home of all campus sporting events and major concerts. Van Cliburn had once performed there to a capacity crowd of more than three thousand people.

But on the night Pat coached her very first college basketball game, the crowd totaled some fifty-three spectators. "There were so few of us," Pat Summitt would later recall, "that I thought rather than introducing the starting line-up, we should just go around the room and introduce ourselves!"

The Lady Vols lost to Mercer University that night by a single point, 84–83. Afterwards, the young coach hand-washed the players' uniforms and began to prepare for the next game. She was working on a master's degree and living off a graduate stipend. She was also in training to overcome a knee injury she had sustained during her final year of playing college ball at the University of Tennessee at Martin, and was hoping to pursue her dream of playing basketball at the Olympic Games in Montreal in 1976 as a member of the USA team. In August 1976, she not only realized that dream; she was the captain of the USA team that won the silver medal.

Her Olympic accomplishments had received significant coverage in the sports pages of both the *Knoxville News Sentinel* and the *Knoxville Journal*, giving her emerging Lady Vols basketball program its first real attention. The Lady Vols started drawing a lot more than fifty-three fans in the old Alumni Gym, and within a few years, they would be playing before thousands at the Stokely Athletic Center.

But now, just a little over two months after returning from the Olympic Games, Pat Head sat not courtside, but in a courtroom as an expert witness in the case of *Victoria Cape v. TSSAA*.

Dorothy Stulberg had approached Pat in the early fall of 1976 and asked whether she would testify on behalf of young Victoria. But Pat proved to be a reluctant witness.

On one hand, she knew about Victoria Cape's case, and she very badly wanted Victoria to win it, for two reasons. First, she had detested the split-court, six-player women's game since the days she was forced to play it in high school. Second, she was trying to build a nationally competitive women's basketball program at the University of Tennessee, and with a limited recruiting budget, she had to recruit almost exclusively in state. Eleven of the twelve members of her 1976–77 Lady Vols team were Tennesseans, and all the young women she was recruiting in Tennessee had been restricted by the TSSAA to the split-court game, leaving the young coach the challenge of teaching her players the skills for the full-court college game.

On the other hand, since recruiting was pretty much limited to Tennessee, Pat Head had to have a good working relationship with girls' basketball coaches at 526 junior and senior high schools across the state. These coaches were almost all men, and for the most part, they favored the split-court game.

And so Pat Head told Dorothy Stulberg that she would testify for Victoria, but that she needed to be served a subpoena. Under the cover of a subpoena, she could always claim that she did not volunteer, but rather was compelled by law to give testimony.

When the trial resumed on October 25, 1976, Pat Head appeared at the courthouse, subpoena in hand. Ann

Mostoller called her new expert witness to the stand and began her questioning by asking about Pat's basketball experience.

Pat responded, "Well, I played basketball in elementary school in Montgomery County. I played high school ball at Cheatham County High School in Ashland City, Tennessee. I played college ball at the University of Tennessee at Martin, and I was a member of the Pan American Basketball Team, a member of the World Championship Team, and a member of the US Olympic Women's Basketball Team."

At this point, Judge Taylor interrupted and asked the coach, "Are you the one that Cheatham County built a monument to?"

Pat Head seemed somewhat surprised by the question and responded, "Maybe. I don't know."

Ann Mostoller then asked Coach Head what position she played in high school. She responded that she had played forward under the split-court rules. Ann then turned the Court's attention to the coach's current employment. Pat said she was an instructor in the Physical Education Department at the University of Tennessee and also coached the women's basketball team.

Ann Mostoller asked her if the university offered scholarships for women's basketball players.

Coach Head responded that at that time, the university gave her funding for a grand total of four scholarships that could be divided up as partial scholarships among several players. But she also offered up a prophesy about the future of women's college basketball. She told the Court that she firmly believed that in the coming years scholarships for women's basketball players at the University of Tennessee and at universities all across the country would begin to increase. Head added that when this happened, she planned to expand her own recruiting of athletes out of state rather than confine herself to Tennessee high school players as her current limited recruiting budget dictated.

Ann Mostoller then asked Coach Head why, if she had the money, she would recruit players from out of state.

At this point, Judge Taylor once again could not resist interjecting his own answer to the question. "To get the best players," he exclaimed, and the courtroom erupted in laughter.

Phillip Condra was not laughing. He stood and objected to this "line of questions," but since Judge Taylor was not only questioning witnesses but sometimes even answering the questions for them, Condra's objection fell on deaf ears.

Coach Head then gave her own answer to the question, stating that since girls' high school basketball players from other states played the full-court game rather than the split-court one, that would be a factor in her recruiting. She went on to testify that the players she recruited from Tennessee had some difficulty in making the transition from the split-court to the full-court game. It was a physical transition, and the "mental transition" was even more challenging. She explained that a young lady from Tennessee who had played guard in the split-court game would "lack the offensive skills, shooting in particular," and that this "would be the biggest factor that might present a problem in going on to college and playing." She explained that because of this, she had pretty much limited her recruiting to girls who played forward in high school and therefore had the offensive skills.

Charles Hampton White then cross-examined the young coach. Being an effective trial lawyer, White chose not to challenge the statements Coach Head had made in her direct testimony; instead, he sought to secure other admissions. Significantly, he got Coach Head to agree that the most successful high school basketball programs in the country in terms of interest, spectator participation, and crowds were found in Iowa, Texas, and Tennessee, and in all three states, the girls played the split-court, six-player game.

He also got her to admit that eleven of her twelve Lady Vols on her current team were from Tennessee and were all "well-grounded in the fundamentals of the game." Coach Head volunteered, however, that ten of those eleven had played forward in high school.

On re-direct examination, Ann Mostoller asked only one question:

MOSTOLLER:
> In your experience personally and as a physical
> education person . . . do you know of any
> reason why girls in the high school age would

be physically less equipped to play full-court
basketball than say . . . college age girls?

COACH HEAD:

No, not at all.

Judge Taylor then could not resist asking Coach Head
one more question: "Do you have an opinion as to how
long it would take the girls to catch up with the boys in
basketball?"

Coach Head appeared confused by the question, and
asked Judge Taylor, "Catch up from what standpoint?"

The Judge responded, "Be as good. Five girls out there
against five boys."

Coach Head replied, "I hope that we cannot have that
happen. I'd rather not see them play against each other. I'd
rather the girls play the girls and the boys play against the
boys."

The young coach then advised the Court that she had
an appointment and would like to be dismissed. Judge
Taylor excused her so she could go on about her business
as a physical education instructor and coach.

But Ann Mostoller wasn't quite finished; she called
a second expert witness. This expert was also a basketball coach from the University of Tennessee. He was Stu
Aberdeen, the assistant coach of the men's basketball team.

Coach Aberdeen was a well-known and popular sports
figure in Tennessee, having recruited future NBA stars
Bernard King and Ernie Grunfeld to play basketball for the

University of Tennessee men's team. (Although it was Pat Head—the physical education instructor—who gave Ernie a D in her course, Fundamentals of Basketball.) Stu was a diminutive man; he was known to guard the tall Tennessee basketball players at practice by hoisting a broomstick over their heads.

In contrast to Coach Head, Coach Aberdeen was an enthusiastic witness. He had strong opinions that girls playing high school basketball in Tennessee were capable of and should be playing the full-court game. He also had an ulterior motive for his testimony. Each summer he ran a basketball camp at the University of Tennessee for girls. At the camp, the girls played the full-court game rather than the split-court version. At the beginning of his testimony, Coach Aberdeen explained, "We offer [at the camp] the same program for all athletes. I prefer not to differentiate between a man and a woman. I like to think they are all athletes, and I train them all the same way, whether they be boy or girl."

Upon hearing this, Judge Taylor once again did not give himself the luxury of an unexpressed thought. He commented, "He doesn't believe in sex discrimination."

Ann Mostoller responded, "Isn't that marvelous, and do you see why I had him come as a witness today?"

The courtroom again greeted the exchange with laughter.

Ann Mostoller then asked Coach Aberdeen to compare for the Court the performance of girls at the camp with that of the boys. Charles Hampton White rose and said to the Court, "Your Honor, I would like to impose an objection here as far as comparison of girls with boys at Mr. Aberdeen's camp. It may be interesting but it has no relevance to this case at all."

Judge Taylor immediately responded, "But the Court is very anxious to hear him."

Coach Aberdeen then explained that he taught the five-person, full-court game to girls at his summer basketball camp because his main concern was "to attempt to teach them all the skills of the game, and the best way that we feel they can do this is the five person game, so they all learn to shoot the basketball, pass the basketball, [and] dribble the ball."

Turning directly to Judge Taylor, he then added, "There is a little difference, Your Honor, in the three person game and the five person game."

Coach Aberdeen then gave an analogy to the Court. He related to the Court his experience as a boy growing up in New York City when his father taught him to drive a car: "I learned to drive, my daddy taught me to drive in a cemetery, but it was quite a bit different when I got out on the road, and when I got in New York City, it was really a lot more difficult because there was much more traffic. And this is what happens in the girls' game as it is compared to the men's game. There is more traffic, and even though a young lady may be proficient in dribbling, the fact that more people are around causes a bit of a problem."

At the conclusion of Coach Aberdeen's eager, direct testimony, Charles Hampton White and Phillip Condra both wisely advised the Court, "We have no questions for the Coach."

Judge Taylor then complimented White and Condra saying, "You both showed good judgment in not examining him about basketball."

This again caused laughter in the courtroom; observers could not help but note that Judge Taylor really seemed to be enjoying the trial.

At the conclusion of Ann Mostoller's proof for Victoria Cape, Charles Hampton White and Phillip Condra called one additional expert witness for the defense. He was James Smiddy, head coach of the girls' basketball team at Bradley County High School, at that time the most successful high school girls' basketball coach in the state. His team had won three of the last four Tennessee state girls' high school basketball championships.

Coach Smiddy was as enthusiastic in his testimony in support of the split-court game as Coach Aberdeen had been against it. He testified that the split-court, six-player format was "the prettiest thing" about girls' basketball since it emphasized defense, as a real tough guard would meet "nose-on-nose" against a good offensive player, and, as Coach Smiddy put it, say, "Baby, bring it to me because I'm not going to let you score!"

Coach Smiddy also testified that the guards on his almost-perennial state championship teams had no trouble winning college basketball scholarships, and that the most highly sought player on his most recent state basketball championship team was Cathy Chastain, a guard. He went on to note that while he personally thought that Tennessee high school girls' basketball was unsurpassed in the United States, there were many people who felt that Iowa had the best girls' basketball in the nation. Iowa, like Tennessee, had the split-court rule for girls' basketball, and at their annual state high school championship tournament, they drew the largest crowds of any such tournament in the country, even surpassing the attendance for the boys' state tournament.

Once again, Judge Taylor could not resist conducting his own cross-examination of the witness. Regarding Coach Smiddy's testimony that the most exciting part of the split-court game was the "one-on-one" play between guards and a defensive player, Judge Taylor asked him wouldn't the same one-on-one feature take place in the full-court game, since a coach in the full-court game would still have to tell each player: "Now look, your duty is to keep this girl from shooting the ball in the basket." Coach Smiddy still insisted that you could not have one-on-one play when you have all the players on one end of the floor.

On cross-examination, Ann Mostoller attempted to question Coach Smiddy about the physical ability of girls to play five-on-five, full-court basketball. Coach Smiddy began to give a long and rambling answer about his experience in coaching girls' basketball for twenty-seven years. Judge Taylor interrupted him, saying, "Let's try to stay right on the point. . . . Coach, you listen to her question and if you can, answer it by a yes or no."

As Coach Smiddy's testimony went on, Judge Taylor became impatient, at one point going so far as to admonish the witness, "You are so full of yourself you can't hear her question." He added that Coach Smiddy should answer Counselor Mostoller's questions "without the long dissertation about it."

At the conclusion of all the testimony, and brief closing arguments by Ann Mostoller on behalf of Victoria Cape and Charles Hampton White on behalf of the defendants, Judge Taylor announced that he would take the case under advisement and issue a ruling one way or the other, hopefully before the beginning of the 1976–77 TSSAA basketball season, scheduled to start just a few weeks later.

The Court then adjourned, and Judge Taylor retired to his chambers. There he met with his law clerk, young Charles Huddleston.

"Well," Judge Taylor asked his clerk, "What do you think about the proof you just heard in the Cape case?" Charles Huddleston indeed had his own opinion about the case, but he was smart enough to defer to his boss. "It's not important how I feel about the proof," Charles said. "Judge, tell me how you feel."

Without hesitation, Judge Taylor replied, "Well, I know one thing. The game the girls are being forced to play by the TSSAA is not basketball."

11

THE SHOT HEARD ROUND THE STATE

In the weeks leading up to Judge Taylor's decision, *Victoria Cape v. TSSAA* attracted national media attention. *Sports Illustrated* covered it in its November 5, 1976 edition, calling it "one of the most interesting legal battles now involving sports." Summarizing the trial, *Sports Illustrated* reported, "Witnesses defending the TSSAA position said [girls'] six-person basketball was a perfectly good game. Cape said if it was, why not change the boys' rule and let them play six to a side?"

The media coverage in Tennessee was even more intense. Sports columnist Randy Moore, writing for the *Knoxville Journal*, said, "Tennessee's most important girls' basketball contest of the year won't be settled on a court, but *in* one."

On the morning of November 24, 1976, United States District Court Clerk Karl Saulpaw put the media speculation to bed by releasing Judge Taylor's ruling. That evening, the *Knoxville News Sentinel* reported that Judge Taylor had "fired a basketball shot heard round the state and nation."

Judge Taylor began his opinion with a finding that no doubt gave the TSSAA hope. He found that Victoria Cape did not have a claim under Title IX because he did not interpret it as granting an individual private right of action. Judge Taylor further agreed with the defendants that even if there were a private right of action under Title IX, Victoria Cape had failed to exhaust her administrative remedies before bringing her lawsuit in federal court.

Judge Taylor then turned his attention to the constitutional issue. First, he rejected the TSSAA claim that Victoria Cape chose to play guard on her team and therefore lacked "standing" to challenge the TSSAA rules for girls' basketball. He wrote, "While the Court finds that the proof does not support defendants' claim that plaintiff chose to play guard, inquiry as to whether she chose to play such a position or had no say in the matter is inapposite. She is injured by the rules applied to guard because she *is* a guard. Having established that fact, she has standing to challenge the prohibition on shooting applied to guards."

Judge Taylor then rejected the TSSAA's second argument that Victoria Cape had no legal claim because a student has no federally protected right to participate in interscholastic athletics. Judge Taylor stated, "The basis of [Victoria Cape's] claim is that solely because of her sex, she has been deprived of the benefits that are conferred upon persons similarly situated. Whether those benefits are characterized as rights or privileges is of no moment."

Having determined that Victoria Cape had a right to pursue her claim, Judge Taylor then turned his attention to the merits of the case: he asked whether the rules imposed by the TSSAA for girls' basketball violated her rights under the Fourteenth Amendment of the United States Constitution.

Judge Taylor noted that the equal protection clause does not require identical treatment for all citizens of the state, and that a state "may classify its citizens for various purposes and treat those classes differently." But a sex-based classification, Judge Taylor ruled, must have a "rational relationship" to a legitimate state objective.

In this case, the TSSAA claimed its legitimate state objective was "to protect those student athletes who are weaker and incapable of playing the full-court game from harming themselves."

Judge Taylor noted that the TSSAA also claimed that its rules for girls' basketball promoted the objective of enabling more student athletes to play the game including "awkward and clumsy student athletes." He further noted that the TSSAA claimed its rules for girls' basketball met the objective of providing a "more interesting" and "faster" game for the fans, insuring continued crowd support and attendance.

Judge Taylor stated that the issue that was presented by the case "is whether a difference in sex of the members of the junior and senior high school interscholastic basketball teams bears a rational relationship to any of [these] state objectives that are sought to be advanced by the operation of the split-court rules."

He then rejected the TSSAA's first and primary contention that its rules for girls' basketball promoted the objective of protecting "weaker and less capable athletes from harming themselves by playing the strenuous full-court game of basketball," ruling that the use of sex as the criteria for achieving this objective was "both under-inclusive and over-inclusive." Judge Taylor noted that there were boys who could certainly benefit from the split-court, less strenuous game played by the girls, and therefore the classification failed to include all of the supposed "weak and incapable athletes."

He went on to observe that many female athletes in Tennessee high schools, including Victoria, were willing and able to play the full-court game. In fact, Judge Taylor found that "the proof established that most female basketball players are capable of playing full-court ball." Accordingly, the sex-based classification by the TSSAA bore no rational relationship to the objective of protecting weaker athletes, including clumsy and awkward girls.

Judge Taylor also rejected the TSSAA claim that the split-court, six-player rules for girls' basketball supported the objective of allowing more players to participate. He noted that as one witness pointed out at the trial, the full-court game often requires much substitution, and depending on how a coach runs her or his team, the five-player, full-court game might actually result in more participation for a greater number of players than the six-player, split-court rules. But, Judge Taylor found, even if the split-court game did allow more participation, classification on the basis of sex was not a "rational means of accomplishing the objectives of greater participation."

The Court further found that there was no rational relationship between the imposition of the split-court, six-player rules in girls' basketball and the objective of sustaining crowd and spectator support. Here Judge Taylor cited the trial testimony of Coach Stu Aberdeen, who expressed the expert opinion that girls' basketball was popular in Tennessee "not because of the split-court rules, but because of good coaches, good athletes, citizens in the state who support their young female athletes, and the considerable tradition of high quality, competitive, interscholastic girls' basketball in the state."

Finding no rational relationship between the TSSAA rules for girls' basketball and any legitimate state objective, Judge Taylor finally turned his attention to the issue of whether Victoria Cape had in fact sustained a significant injury due to the refusal of the TSSAA to allow her to play the full-court game.

Here Judge Taylor rejected the ironic argument by the TSSAA that interscholastic sports are simply an extracurricular activity. Rather, Judge Taylor found, athletics "has become an integral ingredient in a well-rounded curriculum. Thus, any injuries suffered by [Victoria Cape] can be spoken of in terms of a deprivation of an equal educational opportunity solely by reason of her sex."

Judge Taylor found that the evidence at trial showed that Victoria Cape was being deprived of the greater health benefits enjoyed by male players under full-court rules. He further found that due to the shooting prohibition applied to guards, Victoria had "a lesser opportunity to gain a college scholarship than she would if she did play under the full-court rules." The Court thus determined that the deprivation of educational benefits and potential college scholarships to Victoria Cape was indeed a significant injury that deserved a legal remedy.

Judge Taylor acknowledged that he was "extremely reluctant to interfere with the judgment of state officials and professional educators." However, he added, "When a state chooses to deny a significant educational experience to a class of its citizens, and no rational justification for such different treatment can be found, the Constitution requires that such distinction by voided." Accordingly, Judge Taylor ordered that "the rules applicable to girls' basketball which imposed half-court, six-player restrictions and which permit only forwards to shoot . . . be, and the same hereby are, declared to be in violation of the equal protection clause of the 14th Amendment to the United States Constitution." Judge Taylor stated that he would permit the defendants "reasonable time . . . to allow an orderly transition" to the full-court, five-player game for girls.

It appeared that at long last, Victoria Cape was going to get to shoot a basketball.

But in the final line of his opinion, Judge Taylor stated, "The Court is of the opinion that TSSAA and the other defendants will abide by the within holding and for that reason an injunction is not appropriate at this time."

In other words, Judge Taylor trusted the TSSAA would proceed in orderly fashion to abolish the split-court, six-player rules for girls' basketball in Tennessee and allow Victoria and other female athletes across the state to race past half court.

It may have been the only time in his career that Judge Taylor misjudged.

12

OVERTIME

On the morning after Judge Taylor issued his decision, the TSSAA made it clear that it had no intention to make an "orderly transition" to the full-court game for Victoria Cape, her teammates, and Tennessee girls' basketball players across the state. In fact, they did not plan to make any kind of transition at all. Instead, they decided to send the case into overtime.

TSSAA Executive Director Gil Gideon told the *Knoxville News Sentinel*, "Since there has been no injunction, we will keep going like we have been going." Gideon added that he anticipated the TSSAA would appeal Judge Taylor's decision to the United States Court of Appeals for the Sixth Circuit.

Oak Ridge School Superintendent Ken Loflin appeared to wave an olive branch, telling the *Knoxville News Sentinel* that he was not upset by Judge Taylor's ruling but said that he hoped that rather than issuing an injunction, Judge Taylor would offer a "period of grace" before the new ruling became effective. "Changing from girls' rules to boys' rules is not as simple as you might think," Dr. Loflin explained. "I would hope the Judge would give us time to adjust, and the ruling would not become effective until next season."

As usual, Victoria Cape's father, James, was outspoken. He told the newspaper reporter, "If [the TSSAA] appeals, I will fight it as far as they want to fight it! I am happy, very happy at Judge Taylor's ruling. I've just heard that Arkansas has voted to change to five-player basketball for girls. . . . Does Tennessee want to be last in the nation, as they are in education, in basketball rules, too?"

Female high school basketball players soon weighed in on the issue. A poll of girls' basketball players in the Knoxville Interscholastic League showed overwhelming support for immediately moving to the five-player, full-court game.

Meanwhile, just one week after Judge Taylor's ruling, TSSAA representatives met in Knoxville to vote on the issue. Despite the fact that the representatives were overwhelmingly male, the vote was surprisingly close. It was 192 to 172 to retain the six-player rules and appeal Judge Taylor's ruling. So on December 13, 1976, Charles Hampton White filed a notice of appeal on behalf of the

TSSAA to the US Court of Appeals for the Sixth Circuit in Cincinnati.

On December 20, Ann Mostoller filed a motion for an injunction requesting Judge Taylor to enforce his previous order requiring the TSSAA to change the rules for Tennessee girls' high school basketball by January 1, 1977 to allow for the five-player, full-court game. Mostoller argued in her motion that without such an immediate injunction, Victoria Cape would be "irretrievably harmed" since she could complete her junior and senior years playing half-court basketball while the case Judge Taylor had decided in her favor was on appeal.

On Christmas Eve, Judge Taylor held a hearing on the motion for an injunction. Prior to the hearing, Mostoller and White agreed that Tennessee girls would continue to play six-player basketball for the remainder of the 1976–77 season.

At the hearing, White argued that such an injunction would actually hurt Tennessee high school girls' basketball players across the state because "the five-player rule would deprive numerous seniors from playing." Once again, Judge Taylor was not persuaded by White's argument. He issued the requested injunction on December 27, 1976 with a ruling that it would be "effective the day after the girls' basketball tournament ends in Tennessee."

Thereafter, the case was briefed to the United States Court of Appeals for the Sixth Circuit, and on June 22,

1977, a three-judge panel convened in Cincinnati to hear Charles Hampton White and Ann Mostoller argue the case. A hearing like this in the court of appeals isn't a trial, but rather a review of the issues of law presented by a case. The role of an appellate court is not to give a "second opinion" on a case, but to determine whether the trial judge's decision was supported by the law.

On October 3, 1977, the court of appeals issued its ruling. In a unanimous opinion, the Court reversed Judge Taylor's decision, finding "no evidence of any intent [by the TSSAA] to discriminate between the sexes." The court of appeals noted that Victoria Cape had not filed a class action suit, and there was "no indication that the other members of her sex who play girls' basketball under the present rules share in any way [her] views. Nevertheless, she has succeeded in procuring the order of a federal court which imposes her own personal notions as to how the game of basketball should be played upon not only the high school which [she] attends, but upon the approximately 526 junior and senior high schools, both public and private, in the state of Tennessee which are members of the Tennessee Secondary School Athletic Association."

The court of appeals disagreed with Judge Taylor that there was no rational relationship between the sex-based classification under TSSAA basketball rules and a legitimate state objective. Instead, they ruled:

When the classification, as here, relates to athletic activity, it must be apparent that its basis is the distinct differences in physical characteristics and capabilities between the sexes and that the differences are reflected in the sport of basketball by how the game itself is played. It takes little imagination to realize that were play and competition not separated by sex, the great bulk of females would quickly be eliminated from participation and denied any meaningful opportunity for athletic involvement. Since there are such differences in physical characteristics and capabilities, we see no reason why the rules governing play cannot be tailored to accommodate them without running afoul of the equal protection clause.

News of the appellate court decision was greeted in some quarters with elation and in others with derision. TSSAA Executive Secretary Gil Gideon said, "I don't think there was anything discriminatory with our present rules. We had argued all along that [Victoria Cape] was not deprived of her right to shoot because she could play either forward or guard."

The decision came tinged with controversy. On March 10, 1978, the *Knoxville News Sentinel* reported that Gil Gideon "admitted to having an 'in' with the Sixth Circuit Court of Appeals in Cincinnati that ruled in favor of the TSSAA and the six-girls game." Specifically, it was noted that Judge Harry Phillips, a member of the court, was the TSSAA's attorney "many, many years ago." Judge Phillips had recused himself from the Victoria Cape case when it came before the Court, but the *News Sentinel* commented, "Phillips' place on the circuit didn't hurt the TSSAA." Meanwhile, *Sports Illustrated* slammed the decision as "plunging the girls' game in [Tennessee] back into the 19th century."

Dorothy Stulberg called the ruling "unbelievable." "This is disappointing news," she told the *Tennessean*. "I am very discouraged. The judges failed to recognize the problems of women in discrimination."

When UT women's basketball coach Pat Head heard the news, she shared Dorothy Stulberg's disappointment. The coach had been a reluctant expert witness at trial, but she had strong opinions about the restrictions the TSSAA imposed on Tennessee high school girls' basketball players and the impact it made on her Lady Vols basketball program as well.

Ann Mostoller, Dorothy Stulberg, and James and Victoria Cape met and agreed that it was time for a second overtime. They planned to carry their battle to Washington, DC.

13

HEALTH, EDUCATION, WELFARE, AND BASKETBALL

Pressing her case in Washington wasn't a new strategy for Dorothy Stulberg; in fact, she'd been doing it all along. Victoria Cape's lawsuit about the rules of girls' basketball was just one front in an all-out assault Dorothy had launched against inequality in the Oak Ridge school system.

On October 27, 1976—the same week that Judge Taylor was hearing the second part of Victoria's case—Dorothy and two other Oak Ridge residents sent a letter to the chairman of the Oak Ridge Board of Education. In the letter, Dorothy and the other Oak Ridgers—Lee and Susie Shugart—complained of a number of inequities facing girls' athletics at Oak Ridge that wouldn't be covered by Victoria's suit. Dorothy wrote that at an earlier meeting, she had been assured by the Board of Education that they would address the "disparity in quality and quantity of athletic programs provided for Oak Ridge girls as opposed to the Oak Ridge boys."

However, Dorothy argued that far from addressing that gap in opportunity and resources, the school administrators had actually widened it. She pointed out that the girls' track team still wasn't receiving equal equipment, and decried that there was no budget available for review for the 1976–77 school year.

At the end of her letter, Dorothy warned that if neither the school nor the board would rectify these inequalities on their own, she would call on the federal government in Washington to do it for them. She wrote, "It is possible to request a review of our system by the Department of Health, Education and Welfare or to take legal action ourselves. Our preference is for the Administration to take action because of their own personal commitment. However, we are no longer satisfied with verbal assurances of future action."

Apparently those verbal assurances remained unsatisfactory, since on March 22, 1977, Dorothy and the Shugarts submitted a two-page formal Complaint to the Department of Health, Education, and Welfare (HEW). In their Complaint, they wrote that they were "requesting an investigation into the policies and practices of the Oak Ridge Tennessee Public School System in the operation of the athletic program in the secondary schools." Their accusations covered not only girls' basketball, but also the entire operation of athletics at the school. They noted inequalities in equipment, facilities, training, scheduling, and budgeting across all sports, and pointed out that there were only junior varsity teams available for boys, not girls. In short, Dorothy alleged that a "plan has not been developed to accommodate the interests and abilities of both sexes."

Though the Complaint was aimed primarily at the practices of the Oak Ridge school district, it also implicated the TSSAA. The Complaint stated: "The Oak Ridge Public School system is a member of the Tennessee Secondary School Athletic Association, an association which controls athletics in the state, and which recognizes more sports for boys than girls and in other ways deemphasizes girls athletics." The Complaint ended by invoking Title IX, saying that Oak Ridge schools had failed to comply with the law's requirements for "equal opportunity for boys and girls in athletic programs."

Two months later, in May 1977, the HEW sent investigators to do an onsite inspection of Oak Ridge High School. The inspection lasted five days, and the HEW then took another eight months to issue its ruling. During those eight months, the Sixth Circuit issued its opinion overturning Judge Taylor's ruling. Faced with the uncertainty and expense of appealing the Sixth Circuit's decision to the Supreme Court, the Capes decided not to file for further review. The TSSAA planned to vote on a rule change in December anyway, and so Victoria, her father, and her lawyers pinned their hopes for undoing the Sixth Circuit's ruling on the actions of the HEW and on the tide of public opinion rising against the six-player game.

When the HEW's written opinion came down in January 1978, it seemed like they were vindicated in that hope. The HEW informed the Oak Ridge's school superintendent Kenneth Loflin that his schools were in violation of Title IX's nondiscrimination requirements and outlined a series of changes that would need to be made to ensure Oak Ridge's continued access to federal funding. Those changes largely aligned with the Complaint that Dorothy and the Shugarts had submitted: the school was ordered to address their imbalances in equipment, availability of varsity teams for girls, prime time scheduling, and coach salaries, among others.

Probably the most cathartic provision for Dorothy Stulberg was the order that Oak Ridge scrap the half-court game and transition to full-court, five-on-five basketball. Essentially, the HEW was picking up the Title IX charge that Judge Taylor had declined to address, and stating decisively that the six-player game didn't give girls the full opportunities to which they were entitled by law.

Dorothy's reaction to the order was quoted in the *Oak Ridger* newspaper: "It does show that Title IX is going to be implemented. To me it is so important. It doesn't help boys to have a false feeling of superiority or for girls to have a false sense of inferiority. It seems such a simple and basic concept that every person is important."

The HEW order sent shock waves across the nation, particularly in states like New York, Texas, and Iowa, where girls' high school basketball was still confined to the split-court game. Dorothy Stulberg told the *Des Moines Register,* "If it happened here [in Tennessee], it can happen anywhere, including Iowa. We hope the waves we're making will ripple all over the country and help girls to realize they are all important. The HEW order is a major step for women's athletics in the country as far as I am concerned."

Iowa Governor Robert Ray was irritated by the prospect of HEW meddling in Iowa girls' basketball. "If they want equal rights, they ought to make the boys play six-player basketball," he told the *Fort Dodge (Iowa) Messenger.* "You can take everything to the extreme, and pretty soon they'll tell them how many balls they have to shoot toward the basket."

Back in Oak Ridge, Superintendent Loflin's reaction to the order paid less attention to Dorothy Stulberg's creed that every person is important than to the common administrative creed that every dollar is important. He fretted over how much implementing the order might cost, worried because some of the sports it implicated were non-revenue sports, and suggested he might challenge some parts of the order in an administrative hearing. Specifically, he pointed to the change to full-court girls' basketball as one of the points of the order he might contest. The concern was that changing Oak Ridge's rules would put them in conflict with the TSSAA, which still prescribed the half-court game for the rest of the state.

Indeed, during the same months that the HEW had been assessing the Oak Ridge school district, the TSSAA had been doing some soul-searching of its own about the rules of girls' basketball. In December 1977, while the HEW Complaint was still pending, the TSSAA had taken up a vote of its full membership on the question of whether they preferred to continue with the half-court game or switch to full court. The coaches voted—by a narrow margin—to switch to full-court rules. (East Tennessee—home of the Lady Vols and Victoria Cape—voted overwhelmingly for the full-court game. West Tennessee's vote was close. Middle Tennessee—home of past AAU glory and the TSSAA— voted to keep the half-court game in a landslide.)

It's hard to see why that membership vote wasn't the end of the issue entirely. After all, when the Sixth Circuit overturned Judge Taylor's decision in October of that same year, TSSAA Executive Secretary Gil Gideon approved of the ruling by saying that the TSSAA was only looking to uphold the opinion of the majority of its membership schools. "The member schools voted to keep the rules like they were," Gideon said. "One of these days they might vote to change them. The important thing is that they got to keep them like they wanted them." So when the membership *did* vote to change them, just a few months later, it would've been reasonable to expect that the TSSAA would go along with it.

Reasonable, yes, but also fruitless: instead, the TSSAA Board of Control met on March 17, 1978 and voted to keep the half-court rules in place. The vote, which took place three months after the coaches voted to change the rules and just two months after the HEW ordered Oak Ridge to do the same, again broke down on regional lines. East and West Tennessee's representatives largely voted for the change, but Middle Tennessee held the line against the full-court game.

Ted Riggs, a sports writer for the *Knoxville News-Sentinel*, summed up the TSSAA's opposition to change in a column that ran the day after the Board of Control vote: "Lawsuits and threats won't change things, however. Gil Gideon, TSSAA executive secretary, says schools fielding girls' teams will have no options in 1978–79 . . . it's the half-court game or nothing."

Riggs might have been right that it was too late for the 1978–79 season, but he was also forgetting that proponents of change had a weapon even more powerful than lawsuits or threats: they had Coach Patricia Head.

14

THE COACH DRAWS A LINE

Pat Head was not pleased when the Sixth Circuit overturned Judge Taylor's ruling. On October 4, 1977, she was interviewed for an article in the *Tennessean* titled "Reactions Varied Among Coaches." Commenting on the Court's decision, Pat was quoted saying, "My feelings about it are still the same. Defensive players will be at a disadvantage when college coaches look at prospects. And too, none of the players will have the benefit of showing all their talent. The college coach will have to imagine how good a girl, forward or guard, will be when given the opportunity to play full court."

The article also quoted another woman coaching college ball, Tennessee Tech's Marynell Meadors, who felt the decision was looking backward just when the sport should be focused on the future. On the other hand, the article surveyed four Tennessee high school coaches who were delighted to hear they would not have to change to the full-court game. All four of them were men.

The continued grip of that old boys' club on Tennessee girls' basketball was probably why Pat tempered her public comments on the Sixth Circuit reversal. While she of course expressed her disapproval, she did it in the same diplomatic, cautious way that she had expressed support for Victoria's cause at trial.

For instance, Pat was interviewed for a *Knoxville Journal* article that also ran on October 4, 1977. *Journal* sports writer Randy Moore described her reaction to the news as "tactful understatement." She told Moore, "I can't criticize the TSSAA because the six-member game has given us some fine players the past few years. But I feel the switch to the five-member game would be a definite improvement." And when she mentioned the possibility that the TSSAA's stubbornness might someday force her to focus her recruiting efforts out of state, she was quick to qualify: "I hope it doesn't come to that."

But the truth was, the rising star of Pat's Lady Vols was even then rapidly eclipsing the inflexible old guard in Tennessee basketball. Women's basketball in general had been growing in popularity and prestige since its inclusion in the 1976 Montreal games, and nowhere was the sport's ascension more meteoric than in southeastern colleges. According to an AP report from February 1979, funding for women's basketball programs in the ten schools in the Southeastern Conference rose from bake sale-supplement levels to more than $650,000 over the course of just a few years.

The Lady Vols were at the forefront of that revolution. Since her debut as head coach in 1974, Pat made her team competitive, first on the state and then on the national level. She made her first appearance at the Association for Intercollegiate Athletics for Women (AIAW, the NCAA's predecessor for women) tournament in 1976, taking her team to the Final Four. In 1978, Pat's Lady Vols beat three-time National Champion Delta State in front of more than six thousand fans at Stokely Athletic Center, earning Tennessee its first-ever number-one national ranking.

With success came money, which in turn bred more success. That same 1979 AP report put the Lady Vols' budget for the season at $96,000, second in the SEC only to Kentucky. New money meant new scholarships, which according to Pat made all the difference. It allowed her to begin recruiting players out of state, which she said gave the team access to "better athletes" with "far better skills."

In addition to better athletes, the ability to recruit out of state also brought Pat another advantage, one she had been missing during those years of having to kowtow to stodgy high school coaches: leverage. As the Lady Vols became a premier destination for elite high school athletes from across the country, Pat no longer needed Tennessee's coaches to help her recruit a class. She could go elsewhere.

Armed with that new leverage, Pat became increasingly outspoken about her dislike for the six-player game. In her book *Sum It Up*, Pat described the campaign she waged across the state in the years after she had to be subpoenaed to testify in Victoria Cape's trial: "I declared that the Tennessee schools forced 'a mental and physical handicap' on girls, and stumped all around the state, begging parents and other coaches to testify similarly and support a rule change. Women weren't pushed physically, I said; we hadn't tapped into an iota of what we were capable of."

Her campaign reached its zenith on March 3, 1979, almost a full year after the TSSAA Board had voted to keep six-player rules in spite of the HEW ruling and their own membership's vote. That day, another Randy Moore story about Pat ran in the *Knoxville Journal*. The headline got right to the point: "No More Signees From Halfcourt Game—Head." The article began by talking about two conspicuous absences from the top of the Lady Vols' lineup that season: Jerilynn Harper and Susan Clower. Both were highly touted, top-ranked in-state recruits for Tennessee; neither had started a single game.

For Pat, this was proof as unassailable as you would find that the six-player game had outlived its usefulness. "I realized midseason that there's just too much adjustment to make in going from six-girl to five-girl," she explained.

"Jerilynn and Susan are fine players with great potential. But they'd be way ahead in their basketball development if they had been playing the five-girl game all along." And so Pat issued a simple proclamation: "From now on, my recruiting will be from five-on-five systems."

She quickly made clear that her decision wasn't for lack of faith in Tennessee's athletes. It was because she couldn't afford to wait for those athletes to turn into basketball players once they were already in college. She said, "Our goal is to be the country's model women's athletic program. In trying to reach this goal and remain a national contender, we feel it's necessary to bring in talented people with good backgrounds who can help immediately."

Though it was still early in Pat's career, the *Knoxville Journal* article made it immediately clear that when she spoke, the State of Tennessee listened. Less than two weeks after she announced her program's embargo on half-court players, the Tennessee state legislature took action. Two state representatives—Randy McNally of Oak Ridge and Buddy Scruggs of Knoxville—sponsored a resolution in the House to "strongly urge" the TSSAA to change the rules for girls' basketball for its member schools to full-court basketball. Victor Ashe of Knoxville introduced another resolution with the same goal into the state senate; both resolutions were adopted.

The House resolution was widely critical of the six-player game. It argued that under half-court rules,

"Tennessee girls are denied the opportunity to play both offense and defense; and . . . full-court basketball offers a much better opportunity for girls to develop and demonstrate all of their skills because it does not limit them to one side of the court." It dismissed the perpetuation of antiquated rules as a "discriminatory practice."

Representative McNally made no secret about the motivation behind the legislature's sudden interest in a debate that had been raging across their state without their involvement for the past three years. Among the explanations laid out for their position, highlighted prominently was this: "Coach Pat Head, of the nationally ranked Lady Volunteers, has also voiced her support for a change and stated in the March 3, 1979 edition of the *Knoxville Journal* that she would no longer recruit girls within the state unless the change to full court is made."

And with that, the dam holding back change had finally burst: Pat Head's growing influence on the game had allowed her to do with a few decisive words what Victoria Cape, Dorothy Stulberg, Ann Mostoller, and countless others had been unable to do with the full weight of the federal government behind them.

Before the month was out, the TSSAA voted to allow girls in Tennessee to cross the half-court line.

Epilogue

BEYOND HALF COURT

The first full year of high school basketball in which Tennessee girls were allowed to run the full court was the 1979–80 season, about half a decade after Victoria Cape's crusade started.

More than twenty-five years later, Victoria Cape is Victoria Hermes, and the marks left by that old crusade aren't immediately visible to the casual observer. These days her life looks more normal homemaker than Norma Rae; she presides gracefully over a stylish house on the west end of Knoxville. Standing in her kitchen—done in warm olive and beige tones—there are no signs of her role in catapulting Tennessee sports into the modern era. The mugs are monogrammed, the candles are vanilla-scented, and the walls are adorned with crucifixes flanking pictures of Victoria's three grown children. Like Victoria herself, it exudes comfort rather than confrontation.

When she does look back on the case that bears her name, she still has a hard time believing the amount of controversy it caused, even though to her the right thing to do was "just so clear." But with the perspective of years, she can easily identify the source of the pushback her simple Complaint generated. As she explains gently, "I guess we're all resistant to change."

When she was younger, the sheer force of that resistance was enough to rattle Victoria. She had graduated by the time full-court basketball had its full coming-out party in Tennessee schools, but it hardly made a difference to her; she hadn't even come back to play on her half-court team during her senior year. "I decided not to play the rest of the season," she said. "It was personal. It was just something I felt. I needed to get away from it. It was just overwhelming for me."

After high school, she eventually attended the University of Tennessee, where that need to distance herself from her revolutionary role continued. When she asked UT career counselors to review her resume as she started her job search before graduation, they told her not to talk about her court case. She remembers them explaining, "Well, it's just that you look like a troublemaker." They told her that reference to the case would be "a red flag."

Luckily, future generations would look much more kindly on all the trouble Victoria made. On the twentieth anniversary of the first five-on-five state tournament in Tennessee girls' basketball history, *Tennessean* staff writer Jessica Hopp wrote lovingly, "Every time a girls' basketball team in the state of Tennessee steps out onto the court with five players — not six — Hermes' influence on the game is experienced."

That same article also gives a window into how far Victoria's efforts pushed public opinion in the state of Tennessee. In the article, a high school coach from Lebanon, Tennessee, Campbell Brandon, is quoted gushing about full-court basketball: "I never really dreamed 5-on-5 would be this good. But I love 5-on-5. If I had a chance to go back to 6-on-6 I wouldn't do it."

Coach Brandon had also been quoted twenty years earlier in another *Tennessean* article, the same article titled "Reactions Varied Among Coaches" that allowed Pat Head to express her tactful disapproval of the Sixth Circuit ruling keeping six-player ball. At that time, Coach Brandon had said, "I'm for six-on-six because it's a great game and no one has proved five-on-five to be better. . . . It should be noted that the new game would likely have resulted in a decline in fan interest."

In 1977, Coach Brandon — no doubt speaking for any number of other coaches in the same position — said he opposed Victoria's suit because he didn't "think one girl should have so much impact on the rest of the girls in the state." Twenty years later, he was still benefitting from the impact Victoria had on other girls — and other men — in Tennessee.

And in one of those elegant complete circles history sometimes produces, Victoria's three children were among those who reaped the rewards of their mother's impact. All three of them — two girls and one boy — played basketball as children, all three of them by the same rules. For Victoria, watching her kids play "without demeaning 6-person basketball" was the real victory.

She describes the familiar happiness of any parent watching their children play a sport, benefitting from a physical and mental challenge. But for Victoria, there was also something more at stake than just that uncomplicated happiness. "It was also a feeling of satisfaction," she explains, "to have had a small part in elevating the playing field for girls to be viewed as equal to boys in their physical capabilities."

And Victoria was far from the only person who participated in her challenge to the TSSAA who continued to see the case's effects later in life. Charles Huddleston — the law clerk who helped Judge Taylor draft the initial opinion ruling for Victoria — found in full-court girls' basketball a life's calling. After his clerkship he moved to Atlanta, where he pursued a successful career in law, but an arguably more successful career as a coach of girls' youth basketball. For more than thirty years, as the director of the Georgia Metros — a premier AAU team — he's mentored and coached more than three hundred players who have won scholarships to play college ball as student athletes. More than ninety-five percent of Huddleston's players have obtained their college degrees, among them Maya Moore, the future

WNBA champion and MVP who won multiple player of the year awards in college at the University of Connecticut.

Even the cantankerous Judge Taylor himself found it difficult to shake the impact Victoria's case had on him. According to Huddleston, the judge was outraged that Victoria's lawyers hadn't filed an appeal with the Supreme Court—he was convinced that the Court would reverse the Sixth Circuit and vindicate his original opinion. In fact, he was so sure of it that when Ann Mostoller once appeared before him on another matter, he took the opportunity to chide her in open court for not filing a petition. Judge Taylor carried such a bright torch for his opinion in *Cape v. TSSAA* that he brought it up years later while giving a commencement address at the University of Tennessee.

Charles Hampton White continued to practice law for over twenty years after obtaining a reversal of Judge Taylor's ruling in *Cape v. TSSAA* in the United States Court of Appeals for the Sixth Circuit. This "teacher's lawyer" and "coach's lawyer" remained counsel for both the Tennessee Education Association and the TSSAA, along with maintaining his practice in labor management, until his retirement in 2000. He lives in Nashville with wife, Fran, with whom he has extensively traveled throughout the world.

Long after closing the file in the case of *Victoria Cape v. TSSAA,* Dorothy Stulberg and Ann Mostoller continued to be advocates for change and voices for the poor and disadvantaged. Stulberg became the founder and director of the Anderson County Neighborhood Youth Corps and the Oak Ridge Community Action Center, serving for more than twenty-five years as Chair of Rural Legal Services of Tennessee. Along the way, she earned her PhD in collaborative learning from the University of Tennessee at the age of eighty.

A few months before her passing in 2011, Stulberg told a friend that "the jury [was] out" on her life and whether she had been "a friend who loves and relates to others."

She was wrong. The jury had returned a verdict in her favor decades ago.

Ann Mostoller continues to practice law in Oak Ridge with the firm she and Dorothy founded in 1974. When asked about Victoria Cape's lawsuit, she modestly credits the victory "to Dorothy and Judge Taylor."

Of course, nobody benefitted more from the rule change than Pat Head Summitt. Looking back on her recruiting ultimatum that finally tipped the scales for full-court basketball, Pat said, "I thought I was going to get run out of the state when I did that."

Instead, it was antiquated rules and limitations on players that were sent packing. The moment was a kind of testing ground for the advocate in Pat. On the most practical level, stumping around the state for the rules change gave her experience speaking her mind in front of crowds, not something she was used to as a young coach who sometimes still felt more like a player. But more importantly, her part in the victory over half-court basketball showed her that she had gained legitimacy in her state, and that she would be able champion her causes without having to hide from the repercussions.

As it turned out, Pat Head freed from those kinds of constraints was a wonder to behold. During her thirty-eight years coaching at the University of Tennessee, she won eight National Championships and 1,098 games, more than any other coach—man or woman—had at the time. Perhaps most importantly to the teacher in Pat, every single one of the players who completed their eligibility with the Lady Vols graduated with a degree.

Pat was diagnosed with early-onset Alzheimer's disease in 2011; she died on June 28, 2016. It is nearly impossible to summarize what she meant to women's basketball, or to basketball, or to women. But it is possible to say, almost surely, that she might not have been able to do any of it if she hadn't first found her voice in the fight for full-court basketball.

When Pat—and Victoria and James Cape, and Dorothy Stulberg, and Ann Mostoller, and so many others—pushed to let girls run the full length of a basketball court, what they really accomplished was helping women expand the limits on what they were considered capable of doing. Then they spent the rest of their lives pushing those limits farther themselves, and showing future generations how they could do the same.

BIBLIOGRAPHIC ESSAY

Prologue

That Pat Head Summitt—or Trish, as she was known in childhood—was an irrepressible character is a matter of both doctrine and lived experience in the women's basketball world. For this illustrative example of that character, we relied on discussions with those who knew her, including UT Women's Athletic Director Emeritus Joan Cronan and Julia Brundige, who was a college teammate of Pat's. We also relied heavily—here and throughout the book—on Pat's own words from her autobiography (written with Sally Jenkins), *Sum It Up*, which was published by Crown Archetype in 2013.

The rules of the half-court game in Tennessee, as described in this chapter and throughout the book, were stipulated in the case of *Cape v. TSSAA* and so we have taken them from the trial record.

As shocking as some readers may find the casual misogyny embodied in the belief that playing full-court basketball was a physical hazard for women, it is indeed born out by the historical record. It can be found in numerous medical journals and articles dating all the way back to the late nineteenth century. Such articles are summarized in "The Sacrifice of Maidens," by Nancy Cole Dosch in *A Century of Women's Basketball: From Frailty to Final Four,* published by the American Alliance for Health, Physical Education, Recreation and Dance, 1991. Such history of medical thought is also summarized in "The Myth of the Falling Uterus," by Erin Beresini, *Outside,* March 25, 2013.

In her autobiography, Katherine Switzer, the first woman to run the Boston Marathon, recalls her high school basketball coach telling her that women should never play full-court basketball because "the excessive number of jump balls could displace the uterus." Katherine Switzer, *Marathon Woman: Running the Race to Revolutionize Women's Sports* (Boston, MA: Da Capo Press, 2007).

1. The Game

James Naismith's impromptu invention of basketball is such a tidy origin myth that it is always a surprise to find that his thirteen original rules are not apocryphal, but quite real; they can be found on USA Basketball's website here: https://www.usab.com/history/dr-james-naismiths -original-13-rules-of-basketball.aspx.

The evolution of the women's game from those original rules can be traced through physical education manuals published across the years. We relied on three in particular: *Basketball for Women*, written by Alice W. Frymir and published by A. S. Barnes & Company in 1928; *Modern Basketball for Women*, written by Kenneth D. Miller and Rita Jean Horky and published by Charles E. Merrill Publishing Company in 1970; and *Basketball — Five Player*, written by Frances H. Ebert and Billye Ann Cheatum and published by W. B. Saunders Company in 1972.

The history of the game in Tennessee and its supervision by the Tennessee Secondary School Athletic Association can be found on the TSSAA's own website, here: http://tssaa.org/about/history/. Their account proudly proclaims that Tennessee was one of the first states to offer high school athletics for girls, although of course it omits any mention of its own role in controversies described in this book.

Finally, our description of the history of AAU basketball in general, and in Tennessee especially, benefitted tremendously from Robert W. Ikard's *Just for Fun: The Story of AAU Women's Basketball*, published by the University of Arkansas Press in 2005.

2. The Law

As for the history of the law, the Women's Sports Foundation has a timeline that gives a very helpful primer on the passage of Title IX. It can be found here: https://www.womenssportsfoundation.org/advocate/title-ix-issues/history-title-ix/history-title-ix/.

To flesh out the events on that timeline, we turned to other academic sources, including a discussion with University of Virginia professor Bonnie Hagerman, which can be found at this address: https://news.virginia.edu/content /equity-sports-uvas-bonnie-hagerman-explains-impact -title-ix. The anecdote about Representative Green urging supporters not to lobby for Title IX is told in many sources; we used the details described in an article in a 2015 issue of Columbia University School of Law's Journal of Gender and Law titled "Using Title IX and the Model of Public Housing to Prevent Housing Discrimination Against Survivors of Sexual Assaults on College Campuses," written by Shannon Cleary.

The NCAA's lobbying effort against Title IX and the HEW's regulations was extensive. An excellent summary of the organization's positions and efforts can be found in *Playing Nice and Losing: The Struggle for Control of Women's Intercollegiate Athletics, 1960–2000*, which was written by Ying Wushanley and published by Syracuse University Press in 2004.

The Associated Press article mentioned in this chapter was written by Fred Rothenberg and ran in the *Oak Ridger* on November 13, 1974. Its headline was, "HEW intends to see women's sports treated equally."

3. The Non-Shooting Guard

Unsurprisingly, this chapter was informed almost entirely by conversations with Victoria Cape Hermes herself. Where her recollections about how exactly the lawsuit began fell short, it was supplemented by interviews with Ann Mostoller.

4. The Coach

Sum It Up was the most valuable source for this chapter — it contains the most complete account of Pat's early life, including her experiences with half-court basketball. Her former teammate at UT Martin, Julia Brundige, also offered her memories of Pat's college playing days.

5. The Lawyers

The sources for this chapter were interviews with Ann Mostoller and interviews with colleagues of Charles Hampton White, most notably Doug Fisher, Judge Tom Higgins, and Tom Carlton.

6. The Lawsuit

The primary source for this chapter was the Complaint, *Victoria Ann Cape, by and through James Cape, father and next friend, Plaintiff, versus Tennessee Secondary School Athletic Association, Board of Education, and Kenneth L. Loflin, Superintendent of Oak Ridge Schools, Athletic Director of Oak Ridge Schools, Billy Williams, and Oak Ridge High School Girls' Basketball Coach, Sudartha Vann,* filed in the United States District Court for the Eastern District of Tennessee on August 18, 1976. An additional source for this chapter was, of course, Ann Mostoller, the attorney who filed the lawsuit.

7. The Judge

The documentary source for this chapter was *Remembering United States District Judge Robert L. Taylor: A Collection of Memories*, edited by Judge Charles D. Susano, Jr., Court of Appeals of Tennessee, and published by Tennessee Valley Publishers in 2009. The other sources were Judge Susano in conversations; interviews with Don Ferguson, the executive director of the Historical Society of the US District Court for the Eastern District of Tennessee and formerly chief deputy clerk for the US District Court for the Eastern District of Tennessee; and Charles Huddleston of the firm of Nelson, Mullins, Riley & Scarborough in Atlanta, who also serves as director of the Georgia Metros, the preeminent AAU women's basketball program in Atlanta. As noted in the chapter, Mr. Huddleston served as law clerk for Judge Taylor in the trial of *Cape v. TSSAA* and helped Judge Taylor write his opinion in the case.

8. The Trial Begins

The primary source for this chapter was a transcript of the trial of *Victoria Ann Cape, et al. v. Tennessee Secondary School Athletic Association, et al.* Access to the transcript was provided by Don K. Ferguson, who served as the chief deputy clerk of the US District Court for the Eastern District of Tennessee during the time of the trial. Mr. Ferguson also shared with the authors his memories of the trial. Patricia

Brake's *Justice in the Valley* (Hillsboro Press, 1998) was also a source for the chapter, providing an outstanding summary of the trial.

9. Xs and Os

The source for this chapter was the court file in the case of *Victoria Cape, et al. v. TSSAA, et al.,* most notably the defendants' motions to dismiss and the responses filed by Ann Mostoller and Dorothy Stulberg on behalf of Victoria Ann Cape.

10. The New Expert

As with chapter eight, the source for this chapter was the transcript of the trial of the case, obtained thanks to the assistance of Don K. Ferguson.

11. The Shot Heard Round the State

The primary source for this chapter was the opinion of the United States District Court for the Eastern District of Tennessee in *Victoria Ann Cape, et al. v. Tennessee Secondary School Athletic Association, et al.*, Civil Action 3–76–234, filed on November 24, 1976. The referenced news coverage is from *Sports Illustrated* in its November 5, 1976 edition.

12. Overtime

The primary source for this chapter was the decision of the United States Court of Appeals for the Sixth Circuit in

Victoria Ann Cape, Plaintiff/Appellee, v. Tennessee Secondary School Athletic Association, Defendant/Appellant, Docket No. 77–1153 issued on October 3, 1977 and found at 563 F.2d 793 (1977). Referenced news stories are from the *Knoxville News Sentinel* (November 24, 1976, and March 10, 1978) and *Sports Illustrated* (October 10, 1977).

13. Health, Education, Welfare, and Basketball

All descriptions of Dorothy Stulberg's correspondence with education officials, as well as her HEW Complaint, are from primary sources; we reviewed copies of the documents themselves that had been retained by Victoria Cape Hermes.

For information on the HEW's inspection process and ultimate ruling, we relied heavily on contemporary news accounts. In addition to the Iowa news outlets cited in the chapter, we also found especially helpful an article from the February 16, 1978 edition of the *Oak Ridger*, written by Anne Greenberg and headlined, "Board oks Title IX plan."

Finally, Gil Gideon's reaction to the Sixth Circuit opinion was taken from an interview he gave the *Tennessean*'s Tom Squires, titled "It'll Be Six-Girl Basketball."

14. The Coach Draws a Line

The sources for this section are generally cited in the text, largely because by this time we find that the newspaper coverage has become a part of the story itself. After all, it was the interviews that Pat Head gave to news outlets during this time that ultimately sparked the rule change to full-court ball.

On top of the four articles cited in the chapter, information on the successes of the early Lady Vols teams was taken from the appendices of *Sum It Up*, which contain season-by-season accounts of win records and championship appearances.

The particulars of the Tennessee General Assembly resolutions were taken from the resolutions themselves, which were obtained with assistance from the Division of Publications within the office of the Tennessee Secretary of State.

Epilogue

The retrospective celebration in the *Tennessean* cited in the chapter was "The Silver Anniversary for girls' 5-on-5," written by Jessica Hopp and published on March 9, 2005. It contains information both on the first full-court season of girls' basketball in Tennessee, and how players and coaches have reacted to those changes over the years. Of course, any reactions described from Victoria come not from this article, but from direct conversations.

The final statistics of Pat Head Summitt's career are common knowledge to Tennessee basketball fans, repeated as often and as reverently as the Pledge of Allegiance or the Lord's Prayer. But if faith alone is not enough to substantiate these claims in the reader's mind, a full accounting of them can always be found in *Sum It Up*.

INDEX